Hoof to Table

Hoof to Table

A Warrior's Guide to Hunting

Brandon S. Reil

Hoof to Table: A Warrior's Guide to Hunting

By Brandon S. Reil

Copyright © Blacksmith Publishing 2024

ISBN 978-1-9569042-7-7

Printed in the United States of America

Published by Blacksmith LLC
Fayetteville, North Carolina

www.BlacksmithPublishing.com

Direct inquiries and/or orders to the above web address.

All rights reserved. Except for use in review, no portion of this book may be reproduced in any form without the express written permission from the publisher.

This book does not contain classified or sensitive information restricted from public release. The views presented in this publication are those of the author and do not necessarily represent the Department of Defense or its components.

While every precaution has been taken to ensure the reliability and accuracy of all data and contents, neither the author nor the publisher assumes any responsibility for the use or misuse of information contained in this book.

"Then God blessed them, and God said to them, "Be fruitful and multiply; fill the earth and subdue it; have dominion over the fish of the sea, over the birds of the air, and over every living thing that moves on the earth (Gen 1:28)."

Contents

Foreword viii
Introduction 1

Chapter

1 – Preparing for the Hunt 6
2 – Clothing and Gear 21
3 – The Hunt 41
4 – Tracking 60
5 – The Rut 68
6 – After the Kill 79
7 – To the Table 94
8 – Off Season 110
9 – On the Range 119
10 – The Morality of Killing 126
11 – The Next Generation 132
Conclusion 138

About the Author 141

Photo Gallery 143

For my dad, Ken Reil, my son Teagan, and all those who love hunting.

Foreword

One of those memories is my first deer, which happened to be a buck that I killed with a bow that my dad had given me for my fourteenth birthday the year before. I remember the hunt vividly. It was a Sunday morning (I know this because my mom made me promise not to miss church). I was hunting with a friend whose parents had a little piece of property that touched our small town's municipal golf course in Fort Scott, Kansas. It was still dark when my friend walked me into the woods and pointed me towards a homemade wooden ladder-stand that he wanted me to sit in. I climbed up in the stand, got my gear situated and waited for the sun to rise. Shortly after the sun peeked out, a slight breeze was blowing in the direction of where I thought the deer would be coming from (known only because the other direction was my friend's neighborhood).

I didn't know much about deer hunting then but I did know that if deer smell you, your chances ain't good. In an attempt to keep my scent out of any potential deer's path, I decided to move about 75 yards to the north. I picked out a cedar tree, crawled underneath it and began clearing out a couple small windows where I thought my shots might be. It was mid-November, which means the rut is typically in full swing. Knowing

Introduction

this I decided to rattle with my plastic Walmart rattling antlers. God must have really wanted me to make church that morning because within about thirty seconds I had a 130-inch buck at 20 yards. I'm grateful that it happened so fast because I didn't have time to get nervous. I drew back, put my first of three pins on his vitals and released. Looking back, I think I told my dad and my friend that I knew I had made a perfect shot, but the reality was... I had absolutely no idea where I hit him! Fortunately, after following the blood trail through the woods for about 100 yds, we found him lying there dead. That deer is not only significant because it was my first deer, and my dad was there to celebrate with me, it's significant because it started me on a quest that has literally shaped a lot of my adult life.

Don't tell my wife... but a large reason as to why I asked her out my sophomore year in high school was because her family farm was renowned for having the biggest deer in our county. I knew that becoming family was the only way I would possibly get permission to hunt. We've now been married for 23 years, and more impressively, I have lost count of the amount of Pope & Young deer that have come off her family farm, now known as the E3 Ranch.

The love for hunting that was ignited after I shot my first deer, that lead to meeting my incredible wife, has also led to my most meaningful and life-long friendships. Notably, all my window-licking, delinquent Buck Commander brothers brought

Hoof to Table

together through Willie Robertson and my friendship that started in 2005. If any of you have seen Willie in action, you would agree with me that he would have greatly benefited from this book; specifically, chapters one through, well, all of them!

Hoof to Table not only addresses the necessities for giving deer hunters their best chance at being successful, it also highlights something far more important, the one who created these awesome animals for us to hunt...God. While hunting has led to some of the greatest memories of my life, I've also learned that no matter how much time you spend in the woods, how much land you have to hunt or how successful of a hunter you are, if we put our hope in the things of this world (although it might bring temporary satisfaction) it will never truly fulfill you. I believe it's by Gods design that the only thing that will truly fulfill us is living a life of service to the one who sacrificed everything... His son Jesus.

> Adam LaRoche
> Chairman and Executive Director
> E3 Ranch Foundation

Introduction

"And God made the beasts of the earth according to their kinds and the livestock according to their kinds, and everything that creeps on the ground according to its kind. And God saw that it was good. Then God said, "Let us make man in our image, after our likeness. And let them have dominion over the fish of the sea and over the birds of the heavens and over the livestock and over all the earth and over every creeping thing that creeps on the earth. And God blessed them. And God said to them, "Be fruitful and multiply and fill the earth and subdue it, and have dominion over the fish of the sea and over the birds of the heavens and over every living thing that moves on the earth." (Genesis 1:25-26, 28)

Growing up in Montana is a hunter's dream. I was one of the lucky ones. My father was a hunter. And I didn't know it at the time, but even as a kid I was learning what would turn into an obsession and lifelong passion. Some of my earliest memories are of hearing my dad talk the night before about going on a hunting trip, and then waking up the next morning, seeing him gone, and anxiously waiting for his return to see what manner of game he'd bring back. As he pulled in the driveway, his eyes, and the hint of a smile would always give it away. Then he would add to the spectacle of the moment with a loud slamming of the bloody tailgate, revealing his kill. Whenever he went hunting during the school year, I would come home and rush out to the garage to see what was hanging from the rafters.

I've always wanted to be a hunter. As far back as I can remember, for Christmas and birthdays, I would always ask for some sort of hunting weapon – knives, or guns, or bow and arrow. Growing up in the Big Sky State, on our family summer camping trips, I would take these weapons and become familiar with their use. I remember at one point, someone gave me a compound bow with no sight, quiver, or rest. It was bare bones. I made some arrows out of sticks and made it work.

For a young man wanting to be a hunter, I couldn't have grown up in a better place. My family lived in a small farmhouse, situated on an eighty-acre plot, a few miles outside of Laurel, Montana. My parents would work different shifts. And so, when my sister and I got off the bus from school, there were a couple of hours before my mom got home from work. I would always throw my backpack in the front door and head out to explore the woods. I loved being outside. Whether it was throwing rocks, spears, bow and arrow, pretending to hunt, or just exploring. I always knew I was going to be a hunter. The problem was I was still too young. In Montana you had to be twelve years old to shoot big

Introduction

game. So, at about nine years old, I started with small game.

I remember my first hunt vividly. It was a very cold Montana winter morning. I was bundled up like Ralphie's little brother in *A Christmas Story*. My father took me to Cottontail Creek in South Central Montana to hunt rabbits. The terrain was full of rolling hills and sagebrush. Based on the icicles hanging off of my dad's mustache, I'm fairly certain it was below zero. The wind made the tears from my eyes go straight back behind my ears. I grabbed my dad's .22 long rifle and headed up the valley. After a short while my dad said it was too cold and we needed to go back to the truck. But I was bound and determined to get my first kill, and I asked if I could go up a little washout by myself. He agreed and went back to the truck. So, I put my face in the wind and trudged up the draw.

Shortly after I spotted a rabbit underneath a sage brush. He was blocking himself from the wind and catching some sun. His eyes were closed so he didn't see me. I moved closer......and closer....and closer. I was afraid he would open his eyes and see me and then run away. But I had the wind in my favor, and he laid still. I was now within range, and I knew it was time. I pulled the butt stock of the .22 tight into my shoulder and peered down the long barrel, looking at the sights and aiming as my dad had taught me. I placed the front site post on the head of the rabbit and squeezed the trigger. Nothing happened. Did I miss? Should I shoot again? Perplexed, I walked the 20-meter distance and saw that I had hit the rabbit in the head, killing him instantly. I picked up the rabbit and rushed back to the truck to show my dad. He got out of the truck as I came running towards him and I held my kill over my head with pride. My dad, smiling, gave me a big hug and told me how proud of me he was. I was now a hunter.

I realize that not everyone was privileged to grow up as I did. This is in fact my principal aim in writing this book. During my time in the military, I encountered countless guys who all have the same story. "I wish my dad took me hunting when I was a kid." Or "I would really like to get into that, I just don't know where to start." The goal of this book is to take a guy like that through the practical steps of hunting, start to finish, so they too can experience having dominion over the creatures of God' green earth.

There are many books available on hunting and preparing wild game. This book is primarily about hunting and preparing deer – from *Hoof to Table*. As I hope to show, a lot more goes into this process than just grabbing a gun and getting into the woods.

I've been privileged to hunt most of my life. This book was written for those who hold sacred our American heritage. While this book provides the essential tools needed for anyone to become a hunter, more importantly, it points the reader to the Maker of

Introduction

the wild game, with the intent of laying a foundation for life firmly founded on God and His Word.

1

Preparing for the Hunt

When I was a kid, fall was my favorite time of year. Fall meant deer season. Sometimes, if I was lucky, I would even get to skip school to go hunt with my dad. Those were proud moments in my life. It's funny looking back to when I was a kid. It seems all the things your "not supposed to do" are the things that got me excited, like skipping school or church. One winter, my dad managed to get invited on a hunting trip to a place a couple hours from where we lived. We would stay in a cabin and have access to a very large piece of land. My dad was going to hunt Friday and come back to get me for the Saturday morning hunt. Since it was such a long

1 – Preparing for the Hunt

drive, he had to come back really early. I was ready. I checked and double checked my gear to make sure I had everything I needed. My dad had already taken some stuff to the cabin for me. The only thing I had to bring was my rifle and some ammunition. Once he arrived, I grabbed my rifle, jumped in the truck and we were off to the hunt.

We were coming up over a hill as it was starting to get light, and we were going to start glassing. When I got out of the truck, I was gathering my gear. When I went to load my rifle, I realized I forgot my ammo at the cabin. I told my dad. I'm sure he was disappointed. So went back to the cabin, got the ammo, and went back to where we were. By this time, it was well into the morning, and we missed the early hunt. Luckily for us it was a very cold, windy day, and the deer were bedded down.

We decided to go where my dad shot his buck the day before. He had seen a lot of deer in the area. So, we pulled up to a hilltop and started glassing. We saw some deer in a valley and two does ran past my dad about 100 yards away. By this time, we split up. He signaled to me, waving his hands, trying to get my attention pointing at the deer. But I was fixated on a buck that was bedded down that he didn't see. I went prone, found a good rest and squeezed the trigger. My dad was wondering what I was shooting at and came running up the hill to investigate. "What'd you shoot at?" he asked. I pointed down the hill. He looked through the scope of my gun and was super ecstatic. He grinned. I had shot a buck in that same area he took a nice buck the day before! So back to the cabin we went, both with nice bucks.

The Basics

There's a lot more to hunting than just grabbing a gun and heading to the woods. I'm going to cover a lot of topics in this first chapter, but I don't want you to get overwhelmed. This is a book of basics. As you gain experience, you'll have an idea as to what you want to focus on. I don't want to bore you with regulations. There are a lot of rules and regulations out there. So, the only thing I will say on that is, every state is different. Sometimes you can even have extra county laws. Or, in the case of North Carolina, gameland laws. However your state does it, be sure to check with your local and state wildlife office to make sure you're always good to go. Ignorance is no excuse for breaking the law.

There are a lot of game out there to hunt. For simplicity's sake, I will focus mainly on hunting and preparing whitetail deer. However, as you will find, the principles involved in hunting whitetail may be used to hunt virtually any other game. For those who know, though the whitetail is nearly everywhere in the United States, it is certainly an elusive creature. I like to call them woods ninjas. They can move so stealth, I've literally had them creep passed my climbing stand

1 – Preparing for the Hunt

without me knowing it. For this and other reasons, the whitetail is by far my favorite game to hunt. A good way to get into hunting is to get to know about the animal you intend to hunt. As with any notable pastime, the more you know, the more successful you'll be.

Again, we can go down some rabbit holes here, but I'm going to stick to the basics just to get you in a tree. First let's talk about where you are going to hunt... public land or private property? There is a difference. If you are fortunate like me to know someone who has acreage, then you're set. Ask for permission and get in the tree. That's definitely one of the pros of hunting. In North Carolina on private land, an out-of-state hunter can get a landowner tag for two dollars. As long as he has written permission from the landowner in his pocket, he's good for six deer, two bucks and four does.

If you're hunting on public land, it can be a bit of a headache. Mostly due to the fact that there are other hunters out there and it's possible to bump into each other. It happens all the time, and some people get pretty upset about it. Just remember, it's public land. First come, first served. Of primary concern is knowing property boundaries. You don't want to end up on somebody else's property. I once got a ticket from a game warden in Colorado while scouting for elk because I didn't know where I was on the map. Always know where you are!

Hoof to Table

A great way to keep in the know is to use hunting apps like *onX Hunt*. The app shows all the public and private land boundaries, and provides land owner information. Another time I was hunting a spot near Camp Mackall on what I thought was Sandhills Game Lands. Only to find one day when I came to my hang on stand, a note that said, "This is private property, please remove your stand or we'll remove it for you!" The landowner had every right to take down my stand. I was happy for the warning. When I checked on my buddies' *onX* app (I didn't have it yet), I was clearly on private land, and I promptly moved my stand.

Once you know where you are, and have an area you want to hunt, next comes the scouting. I'll touch on this again in chapter three, but it's pretty simple. You find deer sign in areas they're moving to and from their bedding grounds and/or water and food sources and set up in that vicinity.

You should also pay attention to rubs and scrapes. Rubs are when a buck rubs his antlers on a tree, causing a mark. Very easy to identify in the woods. The bucks do this to communicate with each other by putting their scent on the tree, marking their territory. They also do it to rub off the velvet when their antlers grow back. Yes, they do shed and regrow their antlers every year! Not to insult anyone's intelligence, but I have known several people who never knew this.

1 – Preparing for the Hunt

Scrapes are when the bucks scrape the ground with their hooves and urinate and/or defecate in them. Again, marking their territory. These signs give you a good indication there is a buck in that area, and you should hunt nearby, depending on the time of year. Another option here is a mock scrape. This is a man-made scrape. You can simply create about 24" by 24" rectangular shaped scrape on the ground. You can also put some sort of buck attractant scent in them too. This is all in hopes a dominant buck will find it and search the area for him. How deep you want to get into reading sign will most likely come with experience. This is a topic up for debate. For example, I've read a lot of articles talking about when bucks will "tend" their scrapes and rubs. Some say during the rut, some say pre-rut, some say they visit them randomly but come back periodically to freshen them up. I've even read that if it's during the rut and you find a fresh rub (meaning you can see the fresh bark peeled up) to hunt immediately. The best bet is to do your own research and watch "your" deer to see what it's doing.

Weather Matters

The weather is also an important factor. If you're setting up for a specific hunt, ensure to at least check the predominant winds. Remember they change often. I usually check the winds every hunt. Wind direction will significantly dictate where I sit. If a deer sees or hears something they will usually approach from downwind. The rule of thumb is, always keep the wind in your face. Which I always thought was kind of funny, because if the deer are doing the same thing, then they'll always be walking up behind you! But they also say that undisturbed deer usually walk with the wind at their back. I guess it's a crapshoot. Not only are deer ninjas, but they can also smell better than a bloodhound. If you're not taking the wind into consideration, you should.

Rain is another consideration. Remember, the deer live outside. They'll move in the rain to feed unless it's a torrential downpour. So, it's basically how bad you want to get wet versus how bad you want to shoot a deer. For the most part, I'm a fair-weather hunter. Except for the cold, I love cold weather. But as for rain, if it's 30% chance or less, I'll go. The worst part is being in a treestand when the skies open up and you get drenched. But that's all part of the hunt!

To get more scientific, based on my research, the three main things people swear by that affect deer movement are temperature, barometric pressure, and moon phase. Again, we can go down some rabbit holes here, so I'll try to keep it simple. Anytime you have a 10 to 20° temperature drop, the deer should be moving. This is common in the North Carolina fall. I've seen 50° temperature swings in a 48-hour period. It can be 35° one morning and the next day 82° by midafternoon. So while the temperature is trying to make up his mind, watch for those temperature drops, and be in the woods if you can.

1 – Preparing for the Hunt

The rule of thumb for barometric pressure is when it's 30.1" or higher and rising. I've heard it holds true for good fishing as well. Hunting and the moon phase is also a debated topic. The way I see it, if the moon can control the tides of the ocean it could control wildlife as well. God has a funny way of controlling his creation. Deer seem to move in 4 to 6 hour blocks. Meaning every 4 to 6 hours they'll get up and feed or drink before going back to bed. Obviously this varies from deer to deer and place to place but it's a good baseline to work off. Moon phase will affect this because if it's a full moon and the visibility is good, then the deer can be out at night with no issues. Whereas if it's a new moon, they may not move as much. I don't know all the science behind it. Deer see a whole different color spectrum then we do, but that's for another discussion. Again, very controversial if you want to go down the rabbit hole, do your own research on it. The theory that I'm investigating this year is the hunter's full moon. Meaning, the full moon closest to the rut. It was a bit early in late October this year and we didn't get another one until late November. During times like that I plan on hunting all day.

Hunting Platforms

Another thing to consider is what type of hunting platform you are going to use. The main ones being a climber, a hang on, double ladder or single ladder, ground blind, box blind, tripod or maybe still hunting. A climber is a 2-piece stand that goes together so you can carry it on your back. You can hunt virtually anywhere you want as long as the tree will accommodate it. The optimum size for a tree is 12-30 inches in diameter. Perfect fit would be a relatively straight tree with no limbs – at least not for 20 or so feet off the ground. You basically attach both pieces to the tree and "inch worm" your way up to whatever height you want. I usually go about 30 feet. I know my height because the cordage I use to pull up my bow or gun is exactly 30 feet. I find this also helps with scent control and movement.

A hang on is a stand that stays on the tree. It has climbing sticks that go together to create a ladder that goes around 15-20 feet to a seat and standing platform. A double ladder is usually one piece when put together and you hoist it into position by pulling it up from behind the tree, with the help from one or two other guys. It has a ladder that goes up to a seat for two. Single ladder is the same but meant for one person. These also stay in position.

A ground blind is made of a light, camouflaged material, like a tent. You put it on the ground and sit inside. If you unzip the shooting windows you can get 360 degrees. A box blind is a lot like a tree house. Some are pretty elaborate. But essentially, it's a mini house up on stilts with windows to shoot out of. There's also a tripod. Just like it sounds, it's a tall tripod with a seat on top. Whatever option you choose. Just make sure

1 – Preparing for the Hunt

you're safe. We'll talk about strapping into the tree in the next chapter.

Since the military left me near Fort Bragg, most of the hunting I will talk about in this book is done in the southeastern United States. As you may or may not know, the majority of the hunting here is done from a treestand, in a fixed position. Not my favorite, but that's how it needs to be done to be most successful. I've tried still hunting or stocking and it's just so hard because of the vegetation and terrain – thick and flat. Nonetheless, at times I have been successful doing it. Ironically, just yesterday I encountered a mature 10-point buck on the ground 20 yards away.

It all happened like this. It was November 14, 2023, at about 10:30 am. The moon phase was waxing crescent with about 1% illumination. Almost exactly between the Hunter's full moon and Beaver moon. The barometric pressure was 30.29" and the temp was in the 40's. I had just found out I had the morning off work, so I decided to do a day sit. I picked a spot I've never hunted before, but knew the general area, Drowning Creek. So, I grabbed my climber and my rifle and headed in for an all-day sit.

I ventured up the creek, moving excruciatingly slow, looking for a nice tree to get in. I looked for fresh sign. After about 300 meters, I figured I was deep enough in the woods to start looking for a tree. As I stood there, looking around, treestand was still on my back, I caught movement out of the corner of my eye. As I turned my head, all I could see was the body of a deer. He was soaking wet from just crossing the creek. My brain could scarcely register that it was even a deer because it was so close. Then he lifted his head! I couldn't believe my eyes. Twenty yards in front of me was a nice, mature 10-point buck. Unaware of my presence, he lowered his head and continued to graze. Then, without hesitation, I raised my rifle and put him down.

Afterward, I realized various favorable conditions had coalesced. I had the wind in my face. The leaves were a bit wet. This kept my movement quiet. It was also during the rut. With a little luck, all these factors added up and I was successful. I would have to say, on a normal day, that buck would have the advantage. But not on that day. Out of my 13 years hunting in North Carolina, that's the first mature buck I've ever harvested from the ground.

Where to Hunt

When it comes to hunting areas, I'm fortunate enough to have friends with private property. There I can hunt with fixed stands already in place. I also am a member of a hunting club which affords access to about 300 acres. This club also has fixed stands. Mostly, double ladders and hang ons. If I want to mix it up, I'll just take my climber so I can go wherever I want. Most of the fixed stands we have in place are also where we

1 – Preparing for the Hunt

make our corn piles. The deer get pretty savvy to this, so I've actually found that sitting in my climber off the corn piles is where I have most of my luck.

In North Carolina it's against the law to bait on public land, but you can on private land. Again, know the laws of your state. There are several types of bait you can use besides corn. Some guys like to use salt licks, or mineral blocks. But they make a ton of different types of baits and or attractants. I personally don't use this stuff. Perhaps a salt lick here and there. You'll have to discover what works for you.

A word on dog hunting. I don't do it. I never have. So, I'll keep my opinion to myself. But a lot of hunters do so I wanted to mention it. This goes back to the public versus private land debate. There's nothing more frustrating than waking up early, getting to your favorite spot, and then, in come the dog hunters. They'll blow every deer out of an area in no time. It has benefited me a few times, by actually pushing deer to me, but it's frustrating, nonetheless. The vegetation is so thick here in North Carolina, I'd venture to say some deer never come out; hence why they do it. On the other hand, I've heard that sometimes deer don't necessarily leave an area, but they will circle back around and let the dogs keep going. Just something to be aware of if you're hunting on public land in an area where they dog hunt.

Next, you'll need to know how you're going to get in and out of your spot. You don't want to be just out there walking around, making a bunch of noise. Chances are, based on your scouting, you should be close to either bedding or feeding areas. So, you still need to be as quiet as possible. But if you don't have a trail or a groomed path to walk on, and you need to walk through the woods, then plan on making some noise. Just move slower to prevent too much noise. We have big feet and we carry a lot of gear. It's not easy to sneak through the woods. Bottom line is you have to get in the tree. Just be smart and move when you don't think the deer are. Morning time is easy because chances are you are walking in the dark. For the day or evening hunt, however, make sure to check when movement is predicted. Use a hunting app and check the weather. Plan accordingly.

A lot of hunters use a side by side, 4-wheeler, or other type of ATV. There are pros and cons. These are nice when you have a long walk to your spot. These conveyances are especially handy for getting your deer back to the truck. Another pro of an ATV is, you're not leaving any scent on the ground for the deer to smell. As for cons, they're noisy. Mature bucks will most likely move out of the area if they hear an ATV. That is, unless they're used to it. But you never know. Sometimes, it's all a crapshoot. That's why I love hunting!

A word on when to go. If I'm doing a morning hunt, I look at what time sunrise is and backwards plan from

1 – Preparing for the Hunt

there. Thirty minutes before sunrise is legal shooting light. I like to be in the tree at least 30 minutes prior to that. If I'm hunting in the evening, I just look and see when sunset is, +30 minutes to legal shooting light. I usually sit for the last three or four hours of light. However, sometimes, during the rut, I'll sit all day. More on the rut later. Normally, the majority of your deer movement will take place early morning and late evening.

Another important aspect of hunting is letting someone know where you're going to be. Especially if you plan on hunting alone. My uncle Wayne died the way I would like to die, that is, if I had a choice in the matter. I don't know the whole story. I was pretty young when he died. Essentially, he went out alone, shot a deer, had it on a cart and was dragging it out of the woods. He must've gotten tired, sat down by a tree, and had a heart attack and died. His wife knew where he was hunting so they went out and found him and his deer. I've also heard a story of a hunter falling out of a treestand and breaking his neck. He was still alive and laid there for, I want to say, 18 hours. He had a bunch of coyotes and pigs sniffing him through the night until he was found the next day. I couldn't even imagine something like that happening. Bottom line, make sure somebody knows where you're going. And if you change your plans, let someone know!

So, there you have it. Make a tentative plan. Know the laws, find a spot, know where you are, check the weather, tell someone where you're hunting, grab your gun and get in your stand. Sounds simple enough. And it is. But it isn't easy. Again, whitetail deer are one of the most elusive creatures in North America. And no, I'm not talking about the ones in the backyard eating your moms' tulips.

2

Clothing and Gear

Regarding hunting gear, you never seem to have quite enough. I love talking about all the gear. This is where it can get fun. It also depends on your budget. But just like anything else, one acquires things over time and hunting gear usually lasts quite a while if you take care of it. As it is said in the Army, two is one and one is none. Or, it's better to have and not need than to need and not have. I've followed that most of my life, especially when it comes to hunting. Sometimes though, you can have too much gear. Allow me to illustrate.

On one particular hunt, I was on my buddies' 100 acres. I had everything. My four-wheeler, my bag with all my accessories, camouflaged from head to toe, and my climber. I was going to go in deep on the creek bottom. I rode in and got close to the creek crossing and parked the four-wheeler. I grabbed my bag and climber and headed out. When I got to the creek crossing, I discovered the bridge had fallen into the water and I couldn't cross. I was pissed. But what can you do! I went back to my four-wheeler, put my bag and climber down and was going to sit on a double ladder on the creek. It was only about 50 yards from where I parked the four-wheeler. Since I was making a bunch of noise, I decided I'd better use the grunt call a bit. That way, at least if something heard me, it might think I was a deer.

It was about 2:30 in the afternoon so I had plenty of light left. I grunted a few times and got in the stand. By the time I sat down, I was sweating so much. I decided to shed some of my outerwear. I was in the stand for less than 90 seconds and I heard something running up behind me. To my surprise it was a little 4-point buck. I probably should have let him walk but with everything leading up to that I decided to take him. I dropped him 15 yards from the stand! I was hunting with a buddy that day, so I left him in his stand and took my deer to the processor. I got back with enough time to get back in a stand, so I got in a different one with about an hour of light left. Right at last light I saw a glimpse of something, raised my rifle, and there he was, a mature 8 point. I ended the day dropping two bucks and didn't need any of the gear I had brought, except my grunt call and my rifle! Taking the right gear along is important, but there is such a thing as having too much.

2 – Clothing and Gear

Clothing

Hunting in North Carolina, my season begins in September. In early September, my attire is quite different than when my season ends in late December. Needless to say, my hunting attire is a lot different than someone hunting in Montana.

I like hats. During bow season I usually just wear a camouflage ball cap. Once gun season comes in, I'll switch it to an orange cap, and when it's cold, I'll wear a fleece beanie (orange or camouflage depending on the hunt). One of the pros of hunting in North Carolina is you don't have to wear orange during bow season. Next is facemask. I found you can get them pretty cheap online and in whatever pattern you want. Mine are from SA (Soul of Adventure). I don't like to have any skin exposed. When it's hot, the added bonus is it keeps the bugs off. And when it's cold, it keeps your face warm. Plus, it keeps you camouflaged from the deer which is the most important reason! I'm sure it helps with scent control too.

As for clothes, in the early season, I wear a lightweight camouflage top and heavier camouflage pants. These hold up to the thorns and briars in the North Carolina swamps. And as always, I usually wear wool socks, and good hiking boots. Unless I'm hunting in a swamp, I'll wear my muck boots. And for wintertime, I have a full suit which you can put on wearing boots. I just zip up the sides and it keeps me fully camouflaged and warm. It also allows me to put as much snivel on as I need.

Kit

Every hunter carries a knife. I always have mine in my pocket. It's the kind with a belt clip so you can clip in your front pocket. That, or I'll carry a Leatherman on my belt. Hunting mainly takes place in the early morning and late evening. For this reason, I always carry a headlamp around my neck. Do not forget this piece of equipment! I've done it many times and if you're hunting a new area, you don't want to get lost in the woods at night. I'd like to say I've never been lost. But at times I've gotten a bit turned around in the dark.

One pro-tip I recently learned, use your red lens and not your white light when walking in or out of the woods. This is due to the color spectrum deer can see. If it's bow season, you'll want to have a rangefinder on you. Ensure to change the battery every year. Or at least take the battery out after season and don't store it with the battery in. Not only can it damage your equipment, but it'll also waste an expensive battery. That goes for anything that takes a battery. A rangefinder is a must when bow or crossbow hunting. If you try using the old estimate range technique, you might get your feelings hurt. Even a five or ten-yard misjudged distance can mean a missed or wounded animal.

2 – *Clothing and Gear*

Next is your harness. Don't take any safety advice from me, as I don't wear one. At least not in my climber, but I will in a hang on. I'm not going to bore you with statistics here, but I know guys get killed and injured every year from falling out of a treestand. I'm a retired Green Beret, so I'd like to think I cannot fall out of a tree, but hey stuff happens! Just be safe out there.

Next are binoculars. These will be very handy. Especially if you can see farther than 50 or 100 yards. I say that because the woods are so thick in North Carolina where I hunt, usually 100 yards is as far as you can see. So, I don't use them so much. But then again, I've probably also missed a lot of deer because I haven't. Deer blend in so well, and if you're not paying attention, they will walk right by you and you won't even see them. If it's rifle season and you have a scoped gun, binos come in handy. You don't have to lift your rifle up every time you want to look at something. On that note, one of the cardinal rules of gun safety is never point your weapon at something you don't want to destroy. Pointing your rifle at everything isn't a great idea anyway. Consider other hunters. I know I wouldn't be very happy if I knew someone was pointing a weapon at me!

Calls

Regarding calls, there's a lot to know. You can be a successful deer hunter without ever using a single call or attractant, but, as I like to say, any advantage I can

Hoof to Table

give myself over the deer, I will. Before you start using a call, you need to know what it's for, how to use it, when to use it, and why. I am no expert, but I have successfully called in deer. If used improperly, a call can actually scare the deer away. There are at least four main categories of calls: grunt, bleat, rattle, and snort wheeze. I'll hit the wavetops on calls. The following link will go in depth:

https://feathernettoutdoors.com/deer-calling-101-how-and-when-to-use-them/

In this section, I just want to cover the major calls. You can investigate more on your own.

At the basic level, a doe bleats and bucks grunts (On occasion, a doe may even grunt too). A basic call is the fawn bleat. This call is made to play on the maternal instinct of the doe. The bleat is how does communicate. The goal is to mimic a fawn in distress. An estrous bleat is used by does while they are on their cycle, during the rut.

Grunts, rattling, and snort wheezes are done by the buck. The grunt is how the buck communicates. Rattling refers to the sound their antlers make when they fight. Hunters will use either real or artificial antlers to mimic the sounds of two bucks fighting to pique the curiosity of another buck, possibly a dominant one, to come investigate. Finally, the snort-wheeze, or grunt-snort-wheeze. This is used by a

2 – Clothing and Gear

mature buck, usually with a doe, to warn off other bucks. This is probably the most aggressive buck call. Bottom line, if you decide to use calls, just educate yourself. And remember you're also educating the deer. If they come in to investigate a sound, and nothing is there, you just educated them on your call. Most importantly, remember, as soon as you make that sound in the woods, you're alerting the deer to your exact location. So, plan on them coming to take a look. As they do, don't forget the scent cover, and don't forget to be still and keep your eyes peeled.

Weapons

Now, let's talk about weapon choice. In North Carolina, bow season opens first, followed by black powder, then rifle. I hunt all these to extend my hunting season as long as possible. I've been shooting a compound bow since I was 17. My first bow was a PSE Patriot Pro. I had it until I was in my 20's. After one of my Iraq deployments, I upgraded to a Matthew's Drenaline in 2008. I still shoot it today. I usually only need a couple weeks before season to knock the dust off and dial me back in a 3-inch circle 40 yards. That's my safe zone.

I'm comfortable shooting targets at 50 and 60 yards, but I'm not going to send one on a deer that far in the woods (I'll talk about why later). I wouldn't do it, unless it's a wall hanger, and the conditions are perfect. A man must know his limitations. If you're just starting to shoot a bow, you will more than likely need several years of practice before you can do that. I'm no expert or professional, I've just been shooting for many years and I try to stay sharp. You should never shoot at something you're not sure you can hit and make a clean kill.

I also have a crossbow. I think I paid about $500 for it on Amazon. It's a Barnett Whitetail pro. It's pretty accurate. I've sighted it in out to 80 yards and the furthest kill I have on a deer with was at 66 yards. Hunting with a crossbow, you can still hunt during archery season and extend your range just a little bit. Next is black powder. I'm fairly new to this game. I bought one off a buddy of mine a couple years ago and still have yet to kill a deer with it. But it's fun to shoot and I don't have any gaps in my season.

As for rifles, I use a .270 WSM (Winchester short magnum). As to which caliber of rifle to use deer hunting is about as debatable as any other topic. I use a .270 because that's what my dad used and that's what he bought me when I was thirteen. It's a great medium caliber round and it puts deer down 90% of the time with one shot. Again, you're going to have to do some research on whatever caliber you choose but make sure it's enough to put down the game you're hunting. A lot of people ask me if they would shoot a deer with an AR (.223). I always say no. Obviously, it will kill a deer, but it just seems that they run a ways before they go down.

In the south, that could mean not finding your deer. It's just too light of a caliber in my opinion.

For instance, I recently helped a buddy of mine track down a deer or attempt to. He shot a six-point buck on some private land right at last light and needed help recovering it. It was in the low to mid 30's (we didn't have to worry about the meat spoiling) so instead of possibly jumping the deer, he decided to back out and wait till morning. Me and another guy went out the next morning to help him look. When we got there, he was already about 200 yards into the blood trail. He explained his shot was about 60 yards, the deer was quartered away, and he shot it with a 30-06. He thought he hit it behind the front shoulder.

It seemed like it would be a quick track, as there was good blood. But we quickly realized we were in for the long-haul. We had a decent blood trail, but it was only a trickle here and there. The freeze from the night before made the tracking easy as the blood was rethawing, and still seemed fresh. The blood trail took us through several draws. The deer seemed to be moving in one general direction, but once we came into some thick cover, we believe he circled back. We found two or three different places where he bedded down for a time, and at these points we were on our hands and knees, crawling through thorns. Several hours into the track, I had to leave. Glancing on my app, I found we had gone 700 yards straight line from the point of the shot, a little over 1000 yards of tracking, and still no deer. Moral of the story, ensure whatever weapon you're using, make sure you're able to ethically kill whatever you're shooting to the best of your ability. We'll talk more about that later.

Game Cameras

A technological resource that increases the chance of bagging a deer is cameras. There are several types of game cameras out there. I'm not getting paid for advertising, so you'll have to figure out what works best for you. The traditional game cam uses an SD card and AA batteries. You attach these to a tree but every time you want to see the pictures you have to go and pull the SD card to check them out. The newer ones use a cell link. You subscribe to a carrier to activate it. This type will send the pictures directly to your cell phone at the time of capture. Bottom line is cams aren't needed to kill deer, but they're great at narrowing down where and when to go get'em. I haven't upgraded to cell links yet, but I do use traditional game cams. To limit being in the area to check the pictures I usually just check them when I'm going in and out of that spot to hunt. I have an SD card reader that I carry with me so I can check the pictures right on my cell phone.

Plan for the Worst

Everything else in this chapter is all optional. Some of it is nice to have, some of it is good to have. Some of it is just personal preference. I don't use all of this all

2 – Clothing and Gear

the time, but I use most of it some of the time. I like to have all the necessities and comforts to give myself any advantage I can over my elusive prey.

I figure this is a good place to talk about survival kits. Now I don't carry a survival kit, per se, but between my hunting bag and everything in my truck I have almost everything I need to survive for a couple of days. But that wouldn't do me any good if I fell out of my tree, unless it was in my bag. Again, all this will depend on where you're going and how long you'll be gone to determine what you think you may need in an emergency. Being retired Army, it's kind of a habit for me to always have at least a tourniquet and a pressure dressing, either in my bag or my truck at all times. I also carry a compass in the event, my phone dies. So, this reinforces always knowing where you are and which direction you need to go in an emergency.

My dad told me a story about an elk hunt he did when he was a kid in Montana's Gallatin Valley. He was already pretty far back in the mountains when they made their camp, and they went out hunting from there. He shot a 5x5 bull elk about two miles from their camp. At the end of the day, they were on their way back to camp and a big snowstorm came over the mountain and created complete whiteout conditions. He was not prepared, and they quickly became disoriented and couldn't find camp. They hunkered down under the bowels of a big pine to get as much protection as possible. They waited out the bitterly cold night only to find the next morning that they were a mere 50 yards from their camp! Making matters worse, my dad was not dressed for the cold and snow as he only had a jean jacket on! In the event of an emergency or any other crazy thing could've happened, that situation could've been a lot worse. Always be prepared.

Ken Reil. Gallatin Valley, Montana, 1988.

2 – Clothing and Gear

Scent

The typical whitetail deer can smell 1,000 times better than a human. With the right conditions, a deer can smell you a half mile away or more. It's imperative you use some sort of scent control. I'm not promoting anything, so you'll just have to find a good product that works for you. I usually just buy mine at Walmart... whatever's cheap and scent free. There're all kinds of scents... autumn and acorn are popular. Earth is a good one too. I've even heard some old school hunters use skunk or fox urine as a cover scent. The best practice is to spray yourself and all your gear down before you head into the woods.

To get even more intense, a lot of companies make body wash shampoo. They even make laundry detergent and dryer sheets that are sent free for hunters. Some scent covers also double as an attractant. Like Shines acorn cover scent/attractant. I really like this one, it smells a bit like maple syrup! Another product on the rise is Ozonics. This product uses ozone to mask human scent. I recently used it on a hunt in Missouri. Those who use it swear by it.

I started this chapter with a story about not needing any gear. Here's one about using it all! First of all, I'd like to say how grateful I am to Adam Laroche, all his crew, and the E3 foundation for bringing me out for their January deer hunt. It was a late season archery hunt on the Kansas-Missouri line, close to Fort Scott,

Kansas. I was hunting in Missouri, but we were staying on the E3 ranch in Kansas. My guide's name was Russell. Let me tell you, he had ALL the gear! These guys had top of the line everything! I was impressed as I generally get my hunting apparel from Walmart or Amazon!

I'll give you a brief synopsis of my three days of hunting there, then go back to the story. When we arrived, they had informed us that the hunting was pretty slow, nothing of great size showing up on cameras, and they were also in the middle of a drought. I think they were preparing for us to not see many deer. But that didn't discourage me because I know how hunting goes and things can turn at the drop of a hat. Spoiler alert, I shot my buck, the first day, and was the only one of the group who shot a buck during that trip. So that just goes to show you the unpredictability of hunting. Anyway, we sat in a box blind the first morning and only saw two does. That afternoon is when I shot my buck. The second morning I duck hunted, led by Curly and Chris. Those boys know how to duck hunt! They really pulled out all the stops to try to get us on some ducks. It was really foggy so it wasn't great hunting, but we still managed to kill some birds.

The entertaining part was, three of them landed on the ice and Curly ended up having to go out on a paddleboard to retrieve them, as their dogs couldn't get through the ice. For the evening hunt that day, we went to another box blind, where there had been a big doe

2 – Clothing and Gear

on camera every day for five days in a row at the same time. Of course, she never showed up for us. The last day I sat in the same box blind I killed my buck on the first day, because we saw two other large bucks on the field walking in, for 12 hours. From that ground blind, we sat from dark to dark, seeing something like 20-30 deer. But I was unsuccessful on the last day.

So, back to the story. As I was talking with Russell, trying to figure out where we were going to hunt that day, we got a tip from his guide buddy that this particular ground blind would be a good place to hunt given the wind that day. He said no one has hunted there in a couple months so we decided to give it a shot. We needed to be in the blind by 1400 because the deer supposedly were there by 1500. Well, as luck would have it, as we came around the corner at 1355 and began crossing the food plot that the ground blind overlooked, there were already two bucks grazing. Initially we only saw one buck, the one staring at us, snot dripping from his nostrils, stomping his feet, and giving us a pretty cool show of dominance. Luckily, Russell spotted a bigger buck to our left, but I didn't have a clear shot. I could only see part of his antlers and half his body. Before I could position myself to get a shot the two bucks blew, and reluctantly left the field. We were committed at this point, so we went ahead and got in the blind. 1500 came and went and we still hadn't seen any other deer. Then a flash from the far side of the food plot gave me hope. Three little bucks appeared, and they came out and ran across the food plot, no shooters. Now I was getting excited! Right at 1600 from the far side of the food plot, exactly where Russell said they would come from, they came pouring in, literally! All of what I'm about to say happened within 30 seconds (from the time I saw the first deer to shooting my buck).

There were four deer that came out one at a time. And they were trotting straight towards the ground blind. I counted them one, two, three, four. The fourth one was my buck! As soon as I saw him, I asked Russell if that was a shooter, and he said yes. From that point on, I never looked at the antlers again, and I was so focused on ranging him with that fancy scope. As he turned broadside, 38 yards in front of the ground blind, Russell tried to stop the deer but he was too interested in the does to stop. Russell finally had to yell "STOP"! He stopped and looked, I fired. Clean shot right behind the shoulder, bolt went clean through and stuck in the ground. The deer all ran off and everything went quiet. Except for the mild panic attack, I was having in the blind having just shot a nice buck on my first day hunting in Missouri!

Since I could also shoot a doe, we decided to sit for a little bit and wait. That only lasted about 10 or 15 minutes and I had to go see my buck. Plus, since we had about an hour of daylight left, I wanted to make sure we found him before dark. Experience has taught me just because you shoot a deer doesn't mean you're going to find him. Luckily, we waited 15 minutes

2 – *Clothing and Gear*

because we found no blood in the food plot and by the time we got to the hundred yards on the other side of the food plot, a doe blew at us. We froze and heard what sounded like an elephant crashing through the trees. I had a feeling my buck was still going down, so we waited another five minutes or so and everything went quiet. This reinforced to me you should wait at least 30 minutes, even if it's a good shot. That is, unless you see him go down. Once we got there, I saw him about 50 yards away, antlers sticking up out of the grass. Big buck down!

Brandon Reil. E3 Ranch, Fort Scott, Kansas, January 2024.

Now, back to equipment. As I said earlier, we were using Ozonics for scent control. I had also sprayed my clothing down. I was shooting Russell's crossbow, a Mission sub-1, with some sort of elaborate pushbutton rangefinder scope (that probably cost just as much as the crossbow)! We had a shooting stick, the crossbow, the complete Ozonics system, expensive binoculars, of course, the ground blind with chairs and a ton of other expensive gear that Russell had in his bag. Not to mention all of the clothing that we were wearing from head to toe as it was cold (low 20's). I think the point I'm trying to make here is whether you have a little bit of gear or all the gear, you can still be successful at killing deer, or not!

Baiting

A word on baiting. It's pretty popular in the South and it goes hand-in-hand with attractants. Again, check your laws, but in North Carolina, you are allowed to bait on private land only. Most of the hunters I know use corn. You can buy it either shelled or on the cob. That is one form of bait. I've also heard of people using sweet feed. Types of attractants could be minerals, licks, or nutrient blocks. There are several types of powders and liquids available as well. Again, you just have to find what works for you and what the deer like in your area. These attractants are made specifically for food, but there are also attractants during the rut like doe in estrous pee, or buck scent. They even make a buck bomb that comes out of an aerosol can. Deer rely heavily on their sense of smell. If you can manipulate that, it will only increase your odds. Just remember, if used improperly, it can hurt your odds.

Miscellaneous Gear

Here are some tips regarding miscellaneous gear that will help out in various ways. Hooks are useful once you get in your treestand because you'll have all this gear to deal with. Hooks simply stick in and screw into your tree to hang your gear off of. They also make hooks that hang off your stand. These are great for keeping stuff organized in the stand. Shooting sticks these are good if you're hunting on the ground and need something to rest your weapon on. This will prevent you from having to make an offhand shot, which is the least accurate. Also good for when you're walking to and from your stand, if a shot presents itself.

Game bags are good if you have to cut up the animal in the field and pack it out. These are basically cheesecloth bags. You can put the meat in to keep it clean. Drag straps are good to have. If you're not going to cut the deer up in the field, they help you drag it out. Or some sort of sled or deer cart. Fancy stuff aside, I usually just grab the bull by the horns, pun intended. A little brute force and ignorance goes a long way sometimes!

Another great tool to have is a Thermacell. This is great for early season when the bugs are running rampant. They even make a hunter's Thermacell that burns with an earth scent. That triggered my thinking to a thermal sight. Check your laws on this one, but they can be good for locating your deer after it goes down, especially in thick brush.

Lastly, you're going to need a bag to put all of this in. I run with a backpack with a detachable fanny pack. But you can get as creative as you want with this. I also keep an old cooler in the back of my truck to keep my hunting clothes in. I don't ride around with them in the truck so I can keep them scent free. Once I get to my hunting spot, I will put them on. The list goes on and on and on. Bottom line is, find out what works for you, know your equipment, practice with it, use it, know how to work it, especially in the dark, and you'll be successful. Just remember, all the cool guy gear in the world will not guarantee that you'll to shoot a deer, or even see one. But it can help if you know what you're doing!

3

The Hunt

Everyone remembers their first deer. Here's the story of mine. I grew up in Laurel, Montana. Hunting deer there takes one over rolling hills, through sage brush, and deep ravines. I was only twelve, so I don't remember much of the details leading up to it. I do remember skipping church to go deer hunting.

I was using my dad's .270. I didn't get my first rifle until my second season at thirteen. I practiced a little bit. But at twelve years old, shooting a .270 was shaky at best. We were walking up this valley watching the hillsides when we noticed a group of deer way out ahead of us. They moved up towards the top and were about to go over the other side. My dad was thinking they were moving away and wanted me to try and get off a shot. So, we laid down in the prone. I rested my dad's fanny pack on some sage brush to give me a stable platform. If memory serves, they were about 300+ yards away. I took aim on one of the deer and squeezed the trigger. The splash of dirt indicated that I had clearly missed. My dad told me to fire again. After three or four shots it became apparent that I wasn't going to hit anything at this range, and the deer disappeared over the hill. We quickly went up the hill to see if we could find out where they were going. Luckily, they didn't go far.

We found a drainage ditch that ran parallel in the direction they were moving. We hopped down into it and ran as fast and as quietly as we could, trying to gain some ground on them. They were just about ready to go down into a deep ravine, so we made a break for it. We took a chance and ran right toward them. We came over the hill and to my surprise a small buck was standing probably 30 or 40 yards away. I quickly raised the rifle, pulled the trigger. He fell where he stood. I know it may seem a bit cliché, but the popular movie at the time was *Dances with Wolves* so I immediately spouted off with, "put that in your book"!

It was the greatest feeling in the world. My first deer. I was now a "real" hunter. Thirty hunting seasons later, I still get the same feeling when I see a deer. There's an adrenaline dump. Your heart pounds. Your hands shake. Your breathing is erratic. It's why I still hunt.

3 – The Hunt

The closest thing I can compare that feeling to is skydiving. It's close. But deer hunting wins the day.

So here we go. You're all prepared. You have your license. Your gear is ready, and you have a spot picked out. Now it's time to go hunting. The first thing to consider is when to go. Previously I talked about this a little bit but we're going to go a little deeper here. As I stated earlier, generally deer will be most active in the early morning and late afternoon. But this also depends on the time of year, and during the rut, everything goes out the window.

I've already given you my secret formula of what time I like to get in a tree, so we'll just talk about some other factors. In early September bow season, I will only hunt in the mornings. Usually by 9 o'clock in the morning it's already 80° and stays that way till after dark. Sometime in October, I will transition to evenings. What determines an evening hunt versus a morning hunt? For me, it depends on a few factors. Usually what dictates this, if not the time of year (temperature), will be location. Overtime, I've just learned where I've seen more deer moving in the morning versus the evening and will hunt those spots accordingly. You will have to learn this with time and experience. This is where a game cam is a great piece of equipment to have.

You can read endless articles online about deer movement, and everyone seems to have an opinion, and they all think they're right! And in a sense, they all are right. The one common denominator is you have to be in the woods to shoot a deer. How long you sit in your stand depends on you. I usually sit for about three or four hours at a time. I have a buddy who only can sit for an hour or two based on physical limitations. Needless to say, I kill more deer than he does. Statistically, the more time you spend in the woods, the more chances you have of shooting a deer. As I said before, during the rut, all bets are off, and you never know when a deer will show up. In fact, the rut is a good time for you to do all day sits. Just make sure you're prepared. Some people are very hesitant to pee in the woods. They think it will scare the deer away. Maybe it does, but I pee in the woods all the time, and it's never affected me... that I know of! If I have to poop, well that's different. I'll bury it. I also chew tobacco sometimes. So, I'll bring a bottle to spit in. Sometimes I'll spit on the ground. Again, this is a scent control issue, but then again, I've still killed deer doing it.

Now you're in your stand. You've put in all your hard work to get to this point. You're fighting against mother nature and the stealthiness of the whitetail deer. They can see, hear, and smell better than a bloodhound so the focus should be to sit still and be quiet. I'm always reminded of a quote from Fred Bear when I think about this. "The best camouflage pattern is called sit still and be quiet! Your grandpa hunted deer in a red plaid coat. Think about that for a second!"

3 – The Hunt

Don't get me wrong, you can still move around. You just need to be smart about it, and slow. I have a bad back, so I'll stand up from time to time to stretch out and break up the monotony. Yet, for the most part, I'm usually sitting and just slowly turning my head back-and-forth. I can't tell you how many times a deer will appear within 30 yards, and I didn't even know it was there or coming towards me. Being in the Army probably helped as I've pulled security staring at nothing for hours on end. So now you're sitting there and here comes a deer. Now what? Now it gets interesting. If it's just one deer, I will try to keep my eyes on it at all times. Depending on how far away and the terrain, if you lose sight of it, you may not see it again. But do your best to keep your eyes on it, because if you need to move to position for the shot, you want to make sure the deer isn't looking at you. If possible, wait until it gets behind something before you move. This becomes more difficult the closer the deer is to you, especially if there are multiple deer. But whatever the situation, do your best to quietly, and slowly move into a shooting position.

Now, you see a deer that you want to shoot and you're in a good position. Where do you aim? This is another topic of debate. I aim where my dad taught me to aim, and his dad before him. Just behind the front shoulder when the deer is broad side. You might be asking yourself, well, how do you get the deer to turn like that? Well, you don't. You just have to wait. You may not get a shot like that and may have various angles. This is when you need to know the anatomy of a deer, the capability of your weapon, and your capability as a shooter, in order to make an ethical shot.

Correct Shot Placement – Broadside.

Here are a few tips. Taking a shot on a deer quartering-away is probably the second-best option after broadside. But instead of aiming just behind the front shoulder, you'll want to aim just behind the rib cage. This will send your bullet at an angle through the deer's torso.

3 – The Hunt

Pro tip 1. Look for the front leg on the opposite side as an aiming point. Both the broadside and quartering-away shot are good for rifle and bow. The next best shot is quartering-to. This shot you'll want to aim inside the front shoulder, basically between the deer's front legs. But it depends a little bit on the angle as well. You have to almost imagine the vitals and adjust your angle accordingly.

Correct Shot Placement – Quartering-Away.

Hoof to Table

Correct Shot Placement – Frontal.

Pro tip 2. Quartering-to is a good enough shot for rifle, but I would not recommend it with a bow. You have a chance of sticking the front leg bone and or shoulder blade and not getting enough penetration to kill the animal. Or possibly only in one lung and now you're going to have one heck of a tracking job.

3 – *The Hunt*

Correct Shot Placement – Quartering-To.

I lost one of the biggest bucks I've ever shot on a quarter-to shot with a crossbow. It was late October or early November, and I was hunting at my lease in

Montgomery County. He was chasing two does and came behind my tree and stopped at 35 yards. I just checked that spot with my rangefinder, and I thought I had him no problem. The adrenaline took over and didn't give my brain enough time to worry about the shoulder blade. My bolt hit exactly where I was aiming, square in the front shoulder. I heard the definite "whack," and he took off. I saw my bolt fall out of him after about 50 yards, and he disappeared into the woods. It was almost dark but I still waited about 20 minutes before I got down as I didn't hear him crash. When I picked up my crossbow bolt, with lumi-nok, I estimated it went in about eight or 10 inches. It was now dark, and another guy from the lease had come over to help me search. The problem was, after about 100 yards the blood stopped. I searched for four hours that night and about six hours the next day, but never found that deer. My buddy Frank even brought his dog out. We scoured the hillsides. I know that deer died. But in that terrain, without knowing which direction he was headed, the result was not recovering that animal. I don't like the word hate, but I hate it when I shoot a deer and don't recover it. It doesn't happen often, but it does happen. Usually with a bow, so shot placement, and waiting for the deer, are essential. However, a quartering-to shot with a rifle is probably okay.

What about neck and head shots? If you're shooting a doe, a headshot means no ruined meat. If you pull your shot a few inches on a behind the shoulder shot and zip it through both front shoulders, (especially

3 – The Hunt

with a .270WSM) don't expect to get a lot of meat. Headshot means no ruined meat. The only recommendation on this again would be your capability. Deer are quick and they tend to snap their heads around a lot, so timing would be essential. Also, this is only recommended for rifle. Never shoot a deer in the head with a bow. If you don't believe me, type that in on Google images. It's disturbing. Neck shots are also good for rifle. Usually they drop in their tracks. It's a little more risky with a bow because if you don't hit the spine or the jugular. You may not recover that animal.

The goal should be to kill the animal with one shot. An ethical, clean kill. Remember, you are taking a life, one that God created and put on this earth. In respect for the animal, the goal is a quick painless death. Let me illustrate. I was probably thirteen or fourteen years old and my dad took me hunting somewhere near Livingston, Montana. We got permission to hunt on a farmer's field as the deer were ruining his crops. The farmer told us to shoot as many as we could. A whole slew of us, my dad and I, my uncle, and two cousins, and another uncle, went out to do just that. We met with the farmer where he explained the property boundaries and some tips on where the deer might be. Hunting mule deer is a lot different than whitetail. They're more curious and tend to stick around a little longer. You can usually get a couple shots if you miss. So off we went.

Hoof to Table

We got to an area we wanted to hunt and came up with a quick plan and split up. My dad and I were together and quickly found the deer. My dad shot one. We went over to make sure it was dead, and then he was going to help me shoot one. We found some more, and I made a quick clean kill on a doe. We were meat hunting, so it didn't matter if it was a buck or not. Since it was still early, he was going to see if we could get one more. While we were at it, we could hear the gunshots from my uncle and cousins in all directions. I assumed we were doing pretty well. Again, we quickly found another deer and I made a shot and dropped her in her tracks.

After seeing her go down, my dad was going to go check on my cousin who was just over the hill and left me to go check my deer by myself. As I walked up on the deer, I quickly realized that she was not dead. As I approached, she tried to get up, and because my bullet grazed the top of her back, her shoulder blades were coming through the skin as she tried to stand up, but couldn't. This was the first time in my life that I felt horrible for what I had done. The sight of it was pretty disturbing. I checked my gun to finish her off and realized I only had one bullet left. I frantically raised my rifle, and at that distance, I couldn't see clearly through the scope. I pulled the trigger. I missed. The deer was now even more frantic. As it tried to get away, the sight of it made me panic. I started screaming for my dad and running off in the direction he went. I

3 – The Hunt

found him and he came back and quickly dispatched the deer, but not after scaring me for life.

Bow Hunting

One other thing I'd like to address here is something that bowhunters will call, jumping the string or ducking an arrow. This only applies to archery hunting. I recently discovered there is something to this. Since no one is shooting supersonic arrows from their archery platforms, it will always be a factor. Basically, the deer hear the sound of the bow and react by ducking down in preparation to bolt. Much like a sprinter coming off the starting blocks. So, two questions to address here are, where to aim and head up or head down?

First, let's talk about head up versus head down. In a nutshell, if a deer has his head down when he hears the bow string, he will throw his head up, which causes the vitals to drop as he loads his back legs to run. If the deer's head is up, he will not have the same ability to duck as fast, if at all. The point is, never shoot a deer with a bow while its head is down.[1] Next, aim at the bottom third of the deer. Never aim off the deer, in case he doesn't drop at all.

Don't forget about distance as well. This is why experienced bowhunters won't shoot an animal that is too far away. What is too far depends on your level of

---

[1] https://youtu.be/foRCrnljoYs?feature=shared

experience. Hunting deer in the South, I would say 50 yards is too far for any bowhunter. Even with a crossbow you still may only get another 10 or 20 yards. The farthest shot I've ever made with a crossbow was at a doe at 72 yards. I know I hit her, I heard the smack of the bolt, but, unfortunately, never found her or my bolt. I don't have any film of the hunt, so I have no idea exactly where I hit her or what could've happened. Bottom line is, never shoot farther than you can ethically kill your game quickly. So, if you're archery hunting, head up and aim low. So, if you're wondering how to get their head up, give them a 'meh' sound. That normally stops a deer in its tracks.

Some hunters are very selective about which deer they kill, especially bucks. One year, I had the privilege to go on a free veteran hunt in Virginia. I was unsuccessful, and I heard a guy make the comment, "I won't shoot anything under 190 inches." I felt sorry for him because he probably doesn't shoot a lot of deer! On the other hand, his trophy wall is probably a lot more impressive than mine. Some say, "You can't eat the antlers!" Whatever your thought process is, do what makes you happy. I eat deer all year, so I shoot 80-90% of what I see. But I always save a buck tag to the bitter end! Or, if you want to be Mr. 190, then you may be waiting a while to shoot a deer.

3 – The Hunt

Telling a Deer's Age

You'll also hear hunters talking about shooting mature deer, or they'll "age" them. How exactly do you age a deer? I usually ask the taxidermist and they'll usually judge it by the teeth. But with a trained eye, you can get an idea how old a buck is.

1-year-old Buck.

Resembles a doe with antlers. Little muscular tone. Neck and antlers are thin.

2-year-old Buck.

Antlers are thicker and pass beyond the ears. Neck width is equal to face. Thin waist and shoulders.

3 – The Hunt

3-year-old Buck.

Neck is wider than the face. Chest and shoulders begin to look heavier than the hindquarters.

5-year-old Buck.

Neck and face appear swollen. Antlers are full and thick. Body is broad, thick and boxy.

Counting Points

In Montana, where I grew up, you counted by side. For example, if a buck had 4 scorable points on one side and 5 on the other I would call it a 4 by 5. A point must be at least 1 inch. Rule of thumb is, it's a point if you can hang a ring on it. In the South a 4 by 5 is called a 9 point. You also have typical vs non-typical. Typical means they have the same number of points on both

3 – The Hunt

sides whereas a non-typical has an unequal number of points on each side.

As I've said, there's a lot more to hunting than just grabbing a gun and heading to the woods. But sometimes that is exactly what it is. On one occasion, I went out to a friend's field with my son to hunt. We had merely pulled in the gate and angled the truck to give us a wide-angle view of the field. The field is about 100-150 yards across. I fixed my gaze on a low spot. I knew the deer liked to cross a trail at that point. So, we sat in the truck and waited. After about an hour, two does came out and I was able to shoot one. Not the greatest story but I successfully harvested a deer with my son, no gear, and we got to make a memory.

On many occasions like that, I would hunt before or after work. During hunting season, I always keep my gear with me at work. Many times, that's the only preparation I make. Still in my work clothes, having no cover spray, no real calls, just me and rifle or bow sitting in a treestand, and still able to harvest a deer. You can ask any hunter, I guarantee they've had the debate in their head a million times during a season, should I go out or not? While it doesn't work every time, it seems like my least prepared trips usually are the most successful. Why am I telling you this? Because you can't shoot them on the couch! When I debate whether or not I should go, I go.

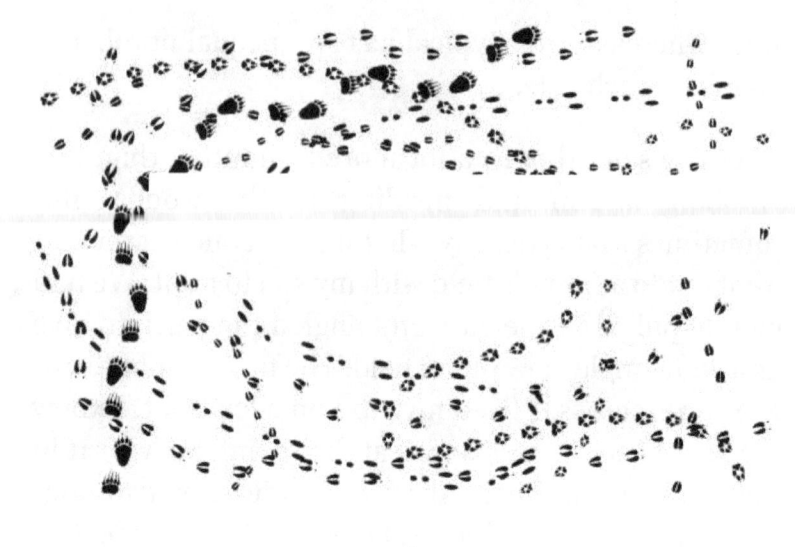

4

Tracking

One of the best things about hunting is sharing your experiences with other hunters. When I was going through the Special Forces Qualification Course (SFQC), I became really good friends with a guy named Rodney, a guy I went through language school with. Two hunters can sniff each other out pretty quick and we did and began hunting together. We went down to Georgia on his family's land and killed a couple deer. We did a lot of hunting around Fort Bragg and Camp Mackall. We had another friend, Walt. He was a helicopter pilot at the time. So, the three of us ended up hunting quite a bit together. Walt had a friend that he grew up with in Kentucky and we were able to go over there and do a deer hunt. We ended up taking my

4 – Tracking

camper so as not to intrude on their house, so it turned into a mini vacation. The weather was cold and rainy, and we were prepared.

We selected our places to hunt, and I managed to get a small feeder field with a pond right at the bottom of some nice hardwoods. I got in the stand around midday. We already put some sweet feed out, so I was ready. About an hour before dark, I decided to try rattling since it was pre-rut. I've never had any success rattling before, but I did a little research and thought I'd give it another try. I banged on those antlers as hard as I could, even making myself bleed and bruising my knuckles, but I was determined. About two minutes later, I could hear what sounded like a freight train busting through the woods right toward me. It got real close and then it got real quiet. A few minutes later, this nice buck appeared on the field. He was looking right at me, but I was camouflaged pretty well in a stand of trees and was able to get my rangefinder on him. He was at 66 yards. I was using a crossbow, and he was in range.

He stood there for what seemed like forever and gave me plenty of time to take aim. I had a steady rest, waited for the perfect moment and squeezed the trigger. As any bow hunter knows, there is a distinctive "whack" sound when you get a solid hit. My hit was solid. He ran directly past me across the field, jumped a fence and stopped. I could hear him moving around, but couldn't quite see him, so I reloaded my crossbow.

He stood there till almost dark, and I didn't even know if he was still there, but I was fairly certain he did not go down. Before I even got out of my treestand, I could see Rodney's headlamp moving toward me. Fearing he would scare the buck, I quickly got down and ran toward him to explain the story. We went to where he was standing when I shot him. I noticed my bolt went completely through him and into the pond and was unretrievable. We could only see my luminok in the water.

There was a little bit of blood and hair at the spot I shot. It was white hair, but very little to no blood in the field. We looked all around the field and found nothing. Worried I didn't get a good hit, we decided to sneak out and come back and look in the morning. There's nothing worse than going to sleep after shooting a deer, knowing there's no blood trail, and wondering if you're going to find him.

The next morning, my two buddies went to their respective spots, and I went to mine. I decided to sit for an hour or two for the morning hunt before I went looking. After not seeing any other deer, I got down and began looking. Again, I went to the sight of the kill, retracing the deer's steps through the field. I found where he had jumped a barbed-wire fence and that's where the blood began. There were pools of blood all over where he was standing. I tracked the blood straight up a steep hill for about 150 yards before I found him lying on the side of the hill dead. I knew we

4 – Tracking

had made the right call. It was a liver hit and it probably took him a couple hours to die. If I would've tried searching that night, I would've scared him over the hill, and we may not have ever found him.

I've decided to do a whole chapter just on tracking, because there are a lot of factors here to talk about and consider. Especially where to aim. If you were like me, and don't have the luxury of filming your hunts, then you will have no way of knowing where exactly you hit the animal. If you've watched any professionally filmed hunts or any of the famous hunters, you know, they have the ability to go back and review the footage to see exactly where they hit the animal. The only thing I have to go off is the blood and tracks on the ground.

Let me start out by saying, you need to understand the anatomy of a deer before you ever intend to shoot one. Knowing the location of a deer's heart, lungs, and liver (the vitals) will ensure a lethal shot.

Hoof to Table

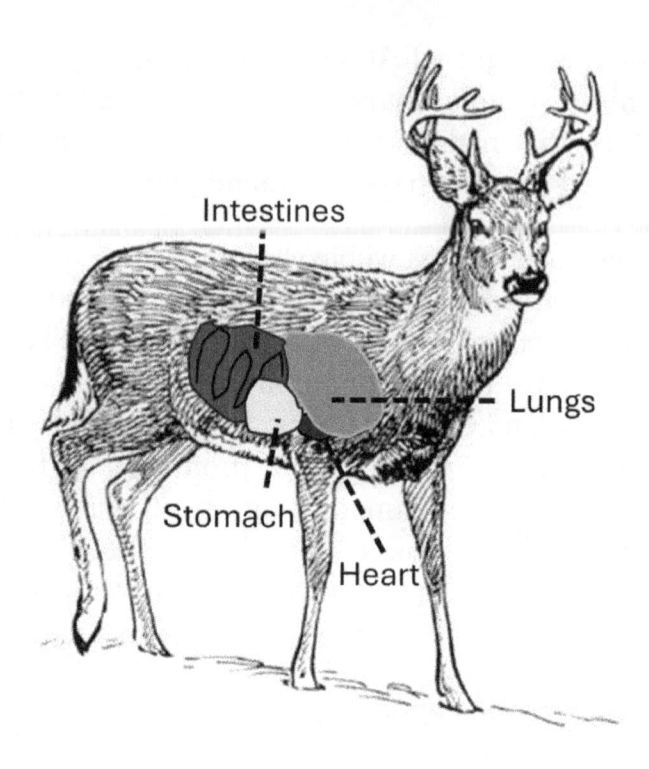

Knowing a deer's anatomy and where to aim covers a lot. But, invariably, at times, you'll have a "bad shot." It happens to the best of us, which is why practice is essential during the off-season.

So, you've made a bad shot, now what? It depends on what the bad shot was made with: bow, crossbow, rifle, or black powder, and if the distance was greater than 50 yards. If it was close with a bow or crossbow, hopefully you can remember exactly the position of the animal and where you hit it. When it comes to black powder or rifle, all you will have is blood, guts, and tracks. You will have this also with a bow or crossbow,

4 – Tracking

but you will also have the bolt or arrow. This is an essential key to the puzzle.

If you find your bolt or arrow, hopefully it's sticking in the ground. What's on it will tell you a lot. If it's green goo, and it stinks, then the arrow or bolt passed through the deer's guts. Depending on the angle, you could still have hit a lung on the near side, and it just came out the guts. This means the animal will still die, but it might run farther than if you had hit both lungs. If the arrow is solid red blood, that's a good indication of a vital hit.

Now let's talk about the blood on the ground. As you begin your search, be careful not to soil the kill site by disturbing the ground. Droplets of blood can easily be covered with dirt and leaves, causing you to lose the blood trail. So, tread lightly as you start looking for blood.

On one hunt, I shot a deer through the heart. As it ran off, I saw blood pouring out of it on both sides, creating about a two- or 3-foot-wide trail of blood through the leaves. Needless to say, that deer was cake to track. However, that's not always the case.

Bright red blood is a good sign of a vital hit, darker burgundy colored red is usually the sign of a liver hit, and that means it will take the deer a couple hours to die. You need to know this because you do not want to immediately start following the blood trail. A general rule of thumb is, if you don't see the animal go down, and you knew it was a good hit, wait at least 30 minutes. Otherwise, examine your blood trail and then decide what to do. Even a gut shot deer will eventually die but it can take up to 24 hours. Normally, they won't go far before they lay down but if you try to follow them, they will get up and keep running, which usually results in not finding your animal. When in doubt, wait.

Oftentimes deer won't bleed right away. In such cases, it takes a little while to find a blood trail. That is why it is essential to watch the animal as long as possible to see which way it is going. I've even had instances where I've called a friend to come over to my location so I can stay in my tree and direct them to the last point where I saw the deer.

Quick story. The first deer I killed this hunting season was a doe with my bow. She came within 29 yards when I hit her. The arrow went right behind the front shoulder. She was down in a depression, and at the time I didn't realize the angle. My arrow never exited. I later found the whole arrow inside her. When I got down to look for blood, I didn't find any or my arrow. As I zigzagged up the hill in the direction she ran, I got lucky and stumbled upon the blood trail. But I only had about 50 yards of blood and then it went dry. And just my luck, at that moment it started raining and I lost the blood trail.

4 – Tracking

Luckily, I had a couple buddies out hunting with me and they came over to help. We spread out to cloverleaf the entire area, and luckily we found her about 200 yards from the shot... no blood... no arrow. They say that when you are bleeding to death, you get thirsty, which is why deer will generally head towards water, or downhill, or both. However, this is not always the case, but definitely something to consider. Or, if all else fails, call somebody that has a tracking dog. They have great success; I simply do not have that luxury.

My train of thought is, if you are going to shoot an animal, you better have the determination to find it. What that means is up to you, but I will tell you this, I've exhausted many hours, looking for wounded deer, and each situation is different. So, know where the vitals are, wait for a good shot, but when that bad shot happens, know how to read the sign and what to do to increase your chances of recovering your animal.[2]

---

[2] Here's an online resource that may help: https://www.whitetailhabitatsolutions.com/blog/whitetail-blood-tracking-tips

5

The Rut

The rut is by far the best time of year to hunt the whitetail buck. You never know what can happen. This story is short and sweet, but it is a great example of how anything can happen during the rut. Sidenote for context: I'm still playing Army in some form or fashion. Since I retired from the US Army in 2018, I've kept myself busy working various contract jobs in and around Camp Mackall, North Carolina, which is the schoolhouse for the Special Forces Qualification Course (SFQC). Currently, I'm working as a contractor for the Robin Sage exercise – the final phase of the SFQC. I'm only telling you this because the life of an contractor can be exciting, but also boring at times. There is quite a bit of sitting around, so we find things to do to fill our time, like writing a book!

5 – The Rut

I just happened to be working on this book. One day I finished up around 1:00 pm and went back to my camper. I decided to do some writing. It just so happened to be during the rut, and it was killing me, not to be in a tree. After lunch, I got my gear reorganized, and did some writing. I checked my watch and decided if I left at that point I could get a solid hour in the tree before dark. I stunk from the day's training, never used any cover spray, no gear, nothing. I just put on an orange hat and drove to a spot where I knew there were some good deer. So, off I went. I grabbed my rifle and my climber and got in a tree.

Funny part about this story is I was actually using my cell phone as a deer call. Youtube has an estrous bleat, or better known as, doe in heat! After about 45 minutes in the tree, and about the third or fourth time I played the call I could hear something coming straight to me. This has happened to me a few times and believe me, when it happens to you, you'll never forget it! It sounds like a bull in a China shop moving through the thick. I got my gun ready, and the sound kept getting closer and closer. Sure enough, a handsome 9-point buck steps out of the woods 10 yards from me. I wasn't ready for him when he stepped out, and my gun was at the low ready. But when he hit the trail, he was desperately searching for the hot doe that he heard.

When he turned his head away for me to check up the trail, I raised the rifle to my shoulder. Initially, I was going to pass, as I was waiting for big bucks, but after a second look, he was a decent deer. Besides, I had just called him in with my cell phone! I had a slightly quartered to shot, but at that distance with my .270 WSM I knew it would be no problem. After the shot, he high kicked and ran directly under my stand. I could already see the blood pouring out of his right side, like a hose, perfect shot. He was down in under 50 yards. Stories like this show the simplicity of hunting as well as the unpredictability of the rut!

What is the rut? Generally speaking, the rut is the period of time when does come into estrus and the bucks find them to breed them. In the Southeastern United States, it usually ranges from late October to early December, with peak rut being in mid-November.[3]

Wait, peak rut? There are different phases of the rut so let's break them down and then go through each.

The phases are pre-rut, peak rut, and post rut. There's more than just these three, but in my opinion, these are the main phases. Let's look at each phase.

---

[3] I found these sites to be super helpful:
https://www.gameandfishmag.com/editorial/avoid-10-mistakes-during-deer-rut/386069
https://www.mossyoak.com/our-obsession/blogs/deer/what-to-know-about-hunting-deer-during-rutting-season
https://blog.redmondhunt.com/how-to-hunt-every-phase-of-the-rut?hs_amp=true
https://www.pressconnects.com/story/sports/2018/10/31/whitetail-deer-rut-fact-fiction/1830988002/

5 – The Rut

Pre-rut lasts from late October to mid-November. Just remember, these are approximations and will differ from state to state and even region to region. During pre-rut, deer focus on feeding, stocking up for the upcoming season. Bucks will start establishing their scrapes and rubs. This marks their dominant areas. They may even begin sparring a bit. Your hunting tactics for this phase should focus on food, maybe even some attractants.

Next is the peak rut. Within this phase, there are some subcategories: seeking, chasing, and tending. Seeking is when the bucks are moving from scrape to scrape and rub to rub (their territory) and looking for does in estrus. Chasing is when the buck is actively chasing a doe or does, waiting for them to come into cycle. Tending or lockdown is when the doe has come into cycle and the buck stays with that doe or does for a time in order to breed them. They say activities seem to cease during lockdown because the bucks stay with the does. Hunting strategies for this phase should include going where the does are, estrous bleats for calling, and even rattling.

Last is post-rut. As daytime activity decreases, deer are now focused on finding food again. Especially the bucks, as they have probably lost 15 to 20% of their body weight during the rut. Bucks are still actively seeking does during this phase, because not all does will get bread the first time they come into estrus. Important to note, a does estrous cycle lasts 28 days.

Since they don't all get bred the first time, you get the post-rut. Strategies for this phase are again, food sources. Hunt over food early morning and late evening.

Since the rut is based on the does estrus cycle let's talk about does for a minute. Consider first the doe fawn. It seems a little creepy to us but it's actually a sign of a healthy deer population when bucks breed doe fawns. They can even get bred and have their own babies their first year of life. Usually around 6-8 months or 70lbs. Wildlife biologists say it has more to do with weight than anything else.

The doe fawns that hit 70lbs in their first year also contribute to post rut. For example, a doe fawn born in March or April that hits 70lbs by November or December will more than likely be bred. They can still be in estrus as late as January. Also important to note, a doe's gestation period is 200 days (time from conception to birth). Now a normal doe is a bit different. First, what triggers the rut? There are many old timers out there that swear it has to do with lunar activity. I think I know why. I did a little research on the lunar calendar and noticed some similarities between that and a does estrus cycle. The lunar calendar lasts 29.5 days, roughly the same as a does estrus cycle (28 days). Coincidence? Yes! So, what triggers it? A little word called photoperiodism. Or as the dictionary defines it as, the response of an organism to seasonal changes in day length. So, while

5 – The Rut

it may seem to line up with the moon, and it may, that's not the reason. It's the amount of daylight in a day. As you know, days get shorter going into winter. But also note that a normal doe can have a variety of other factors too like past encounters, healthy or unhealthy buck population, proper nutrition and diet etc. The point is there's not a 1+1=2 formula here. It's science not math.

Going a bit deeper, I can tell you this with certainty, if your time is limited, or you can only hunt a few times a year, it better be during the rut. At least if you're trying to successfully harvest a mature whitetail buck.

As mentioned before, pre-rut is around late October to mid-November. Now is when to pay attention to strategies and use the science. The bucks are now transitioning from their regular patterns to rut behavior. We already talked about the October lull. There's no lull, the bucks are just deep in the woods doing their thing. As for strategies, focus on food. You have to already know where they eat and where they bed. He's going to be fattening himself in preparation for the rut so now's when to hunt those acorns close to and between bedding areas. Most productive hunting would probably be evening hunts.

I also mentioned attractants. I like to use cob corn and salt licks. You can really use whatever you want, or what your deer like, to help tempt their bellies! Also, don't waste your time calling or rattling quite yet. At least I don't. As I said earlier, if you're not doing it right it can hurt rather than help. And I don't know about you, but I don't need anything hurting my hunting!

Now for peak rut. This is late October to late November. Remember, there's a lot going on here as far as seeking, chasing, and tending but I'm going to treat it as one phase for ease of explanation. This phase is why I said if you can get in the woods. If its late rut, do it now! This phase is when bucks will disregard most instincts, except one. They will go places they don't usually go and do things they don't normally do when searching for some action. So, we hunters capitalize on this.

During peak rut, you will typically see more daytime activity. This is why a lot of rut hunters will sit 10am-2pm instead of traditional morning and evening sits. But if you can stand it, and I've done it, sit from dark to dark. The bucks will be busy. They'll be fighting other bucks to maintain dominance, check scrapes and rubs for fresh scent, chasing does to "check" if they're ready to breed; and when they are, lockdown.

One thing I failed to mention earlier is the length of time a doe is actually in heat. That buck has 24-36 hours to do what he needs to do then go find another one. One buck can breed as many as 40-50 does in one season (dependent on several environmental factors). I mentioned strategies for this phase but anytime you can be in the woods is great. Plus, now is the time to

5 – The Rut

work on your calling. Try using an estrus bleat, buck grunt and even rattling. But go where the does are and don't forget to check game cams to see what bucks are lurking around. I shared the story already, but just to reiterate, the only successful buck I've rattled in was in Kentucky. That was in early November. And boy, did he come in hot! Just ensure you do your research and practice, practice, practice!

Finally, there is post rut, or, as some call it, second rut. I hate to even use that word, there is one rut a season and now you know it's based on the does estrus cycle. If they don't get bred, they go out and come back in 28 days later. Repeat until bred. Most does get bred. Only in rare circumstances will a bred doe not give birth. Some say when does get old they can't conceive anymore. It's called a dry doe. That's just simply an old wives' tale. At any rate you can still be successful harvesting a buck as they're still on the hunt themselves. However, post rut can be the hardest phase to hunt. Don't forget, you and every other redneck in the country have been slaying Bambi for some time now, so don't think this hasn't affected anything.

Also, don't forget about the weather. The late season archery hunt I just did in Kansas is a testament to that. It was cold and they were in a drought. As a visitor, the first thing I was told was don't expect to see a lot of big bucks. "They just aren't moving right now," they said. Just remember, in post rut, they've just lost a lot of weight and need to gain it back. So, focus on food sources. In the South everything starts dying off in December. So now is when I corn it up! And keep using those attractants if they're working. But go back to hunting mornings and evenings as daytime activity will be decreasing. The best advice I can give to hunting the rut, get in a tree! You can't shoot 'em on the couch!

Common Mistakes to Avoid

I want to finish this chapter by mentioning a few common mistakes to avoid. Remember, these tactics are for rut hunting.

1. Don't hunt memories.

If your grandpa killed a monster buck down in the holler 30 years ago, that doesn't mean there are still deer there. Rely on scouting and game cams to tell you what's there, not memories.

2. Under calling.

If you do it wrong or too much you can blow it. This is true all the time, not just during the rut. Remember, during the rut all bets are off. Now is the time to use what you've been practicing. Don't be afraid to blind call if you're not seeing anything. And if you do see a nice buck but he's not headed your way, maybe try the ol snort wheeze. Don't forget, that's the Hail Mary of deer calls, so don't be shy.

3. Misuse of scents.

Don't forget that deer can smell better than a bloodhound. You don't need a gallon of scent to be effective. Also, you get what you pay for. I use the stuff at Walmart so that probably explains why I don't ever get anything when I use scents! Also, if you're using estrus outside the rut then you're not using it correctly.

4. Not hunting water sources.

I haven't really talked about water a lot but it's just as important as food. Especially during the rut. A buck is going to need to drink a lot of water to maintain his pace. Don't overlook hunting near water during the rut, especially if you have an isolated water source.

5. Leaving your stand too early.

I mentioned this one earlier. Obviously not everyone has the luxury of sitting in a tree all day. Especially multiple times. But if you can, do it. If you don't, hunt as long as you can. Don't be that guy who gets in at 6am, in the dark, and then leaves at 9 or 10 because he didn't see anything. Nowhere in this book did I say deer hunting is easy! Even if you have to get out of the stand to take a dump, don't think your hunt is over. Do what you have to do, then get back in the stand. Just don't forget your weapon! I have actually spooked a deer while taking care of business!

6. Not using decoys.

I didn't mention this earlier as I have never used one. However, I didn't want to leave it out as an option for you to try. Based on my research, decoys used properly can be very effective.

7. Dodging the weather.

As discussed earlier, deer will move in bad weather, especially during the rut. Use the barometric pressure tip (30.1 and up) and get in the stand. Plus, if you're too scared to get a little cold and wet, you probably aren't a real deer hunter!

6

After the Kill

One of the most exciting parts about deer hunting is talking to other deer hunters. It doesn't take us long to find each other in a crowd. When my ex-wife was pregnant with my son, we were at the hospital for birthing class. There was another couple there and within five minutes we figured out that we were both deer hunters. I've been hunting with Will for the last nine years. They were locals and lived in the area and had several hundred acres of hunting land. The first time I ever killed a deer on their land was quite an experience. I went with him and another buddy, so we could cover more ground. I ended up sitting on the edge of a field in a ladder stand with a very good field of view, just off of a swamp and right next to the creek.

It was a treacherous walk in. We had to walk through the swamp to get there. Luckily, we did it during the day and we were at least a half a mile from the truck. In the back of my mind, I was thinking, man, if I shoot something back here it's going to be fun getting it back to the truck! There were no trails or roads where I was. A couple hours into the hunt, maybe 45 minutes or an hour before dark, three deer stepped out into the field.

I watched them for several minutes and picked out the lead doe. The other two does with her were pretty good size as well and I thought if I could get a second shot, I might as well try and double up. The .270 Winchester I was using was the one my dad bought me when I was 13. I've killed a lot of deer with that rifle. Hopefully, one day my son will too. I waited for the lead doe to turn broadside. I had a perfect rest from the crossbar of the treestand. I took aim and squeezed the trigger. She dropped in her tracks. I quickly worked the bolt, took aim on the second deer that was still standing there and pulled the trigger again. Instinctively, I

6 – After the Kill

worked both again and quickly found the third deer, which also was still standing there. I fired a third shot.

Usually, deer hit with that .270 will drop them in their tracks but sometimes they still run a little ways, but I didn't see anything. I wasn't 100% sure about the second two deer though. It was about 150 yard shot so I waited about 20 minutes and then climbed down. I approached the spot where I saw the first deer go down. I looked around and saw all three deer within about 20 yards of each other. Three shots, three kills! I was super excited, and I text my other two buddies and told them of my success. It was now going to take all three of us to get these deer back to the truck. As not to ruin their hunt, I told them to wait until dark and then meet me at my treestand.

By this time, it was dark, raining, and I could hear the howling of coyotes getting closer and closer. It took at least an hour for my two buddies to show up at my treestand. Luckily, the coyotes never made it over. We assessed the situation and decided it would be a lot easier to take them down to the creek and float them out rather than try to drag three deer through the swamp in the dark. It was a longer route, but an easier one. So, we each grabbed a deer and started making our way to the creek. With rifles slung and headlamps on, we trudged through the waist deep water for about an hour and a half pulling the deer over logs and around obstacles, making it back to the road. It was then a quick walk back up to the trucks and we got all three deer into the truck.

I absolutely love this picture Will drew for me. It describes the story of our "deer rafts." He presented to me as a retirement gift, forever capturing my first "Lee Harvey."

6 – After the Kill

The first thing I do after a kill is thank God for providing me with meat. My dad taught me this on my very first deer hunt and I'm glad he instilled that in me from a young age. I may forget sometimes, but I try to always remember to thank God for providing for me and my family.

Now, this is the part of hunting you don't read in most magazines! Once that deer hits the ground, the work begins, and you're on the clock. Meaning you only have so much time until the meat can spoil. Hunting mainly in North Carolina, especially early bow season, the temperature can still be in the 80s. Besides that, it's pretty humid here. I like to have my deer in the cooler in at least two hours from the time it hits the ground. Later in the season, or when it's colder, they can lay a bit longer.

In the last chapter, we talked about tracking. Again, reinforcing the importance of a clean kill, if you gut shoot a deer when it's 85° outside and it dies in the middle of the night, chances are you just lost all of the meat even if you recover the deer. A good rule of thumb is, if it's over 40° bacteria will start to grow on meat within the first several hours. When I was a kid in Montana hunting in subzero temperatures, it was not uncommon to let one hang overnight before taking care of it. Bottom line is, know the time and the temperatures for where you are and how long the animal has been laying before you've removed the guts. Use your best judgment.

For years I was spoiled. I just took all my deer to the processor. Main reason was my ex-wife didn't want to see any of that. So out of respect for her I kept it out of the house. It was a tad bit expensive, but very convenient. During those years, I didn't worry too much about spoiling deer as I just threw them in the truck and dropped them off at the processor. But now to try to save money and hone my skills, I do a lot of it myself. My processor makes tasty snack sticks, so I still take some deer in!

The first thing you want to do once you recover your deer is remove the guts (after punching your tag of course). I think this is a fun chapter because I've never actually said this stuff out loud before. It may seem kind of gruesome. Reader beware!

Gutting

There are several methods out there. This is just the way I do it. I start by slitting the throat, ensuring the windpipe is severed to ensure I can pull it through later. Next, I insert my knife blade just outside the rectum and cut in as deep as my blade is and cut around the rectum. This will ensure that it comes out the other side. Then, depending on whether the deer is on the ground or hanging, I prefer it on the ground for gutting and hanging for skinning. I'll cut around the front legs at the bend in the leg. Cut through the skin. Then, going back to find the knuckle, sever the tendons. Then I usually just pop it off my knee and snap the leg in half.

6 – After the Kill

Then, I cut off the leg with my knife. Then do the other side. Next, move up and cut the skin around the hind legs. I use an outdoor edge swing blade. At this point, I will use the gut hook from the hind leg and run to the center, testicles if it's a buck or milk sack if it's a doe, on both sides.

Cut that out of your way ensuring not to cut the pee sack! At this point, you can make a small incision at the bottom of the pelvis just small enough to fit your blade tip ensuring you don't cut the guts. I will then insert two fingers as a guide with my gut hook. And you should be able to slide it all the way to the bottom of the sternum. This will open up the deer and expose all the guts. On the smaller deer here in North Carolina, I can push right through the brisket with my gut hook.

If not, you may have to use a saw if it's a bigger deer to saw the brisket, if you want to, this is when I will reach up into the cavity of the deer, grab the esophagus that I already cut, and pull down. You may have to cut here and there, especially around the diaphragm, but at this point everything should just pull right out. Back up at the top you can reach through and pull the rectum through the hole in the pelvis. At this point the deer is gutted. Now all you need to do is rinse it out with a hose and you're done! This part usually takes me about 10 minutes. It's also nice if you have a buddy holding a leg and helping out.

My deer processor has it down to probably 3-4 minutes. He does his hanging using a gambrel. I don't think I mentioned this piece of equipment in the chapter on clothing and equipment. It is invaluable if you plan on gutting or skinning your deer in the field. It's basically just a piece of steel that you tie rope to, you can throw it over a branch and string up your game. You simply make a small cut between the deer's back leg and Achilles tendon and slip it in.

Again, if the temperature is above 40°, you'll want to get the guts out as soon as possible. If it's 40° or below, once you get the guts out, you now have the option to let your animal hang, depending on how you're going to age the meat. I like to let my deer age for at least a week before I process them. I have an old fridge in my garage that I use to hang them, and I usually will skin my deer before I age them.

Skinning

Next is skinning. This part is pretty straightforward and easy since you've already cut around all four legs earlier. Now it's just a matter of taking your knife and peeling back the skin, usually from top to bottom.

Pro-tip #1. Once you get it started generally you can just grab a hold of the skin and push/pull down and it will just peel all the way down to the neck.

Pro-tip #2. Cut up to the chest cavity on the front legs before you get all the skin down on top of it, otherwise,

6 – After the Kill

you'll have a hard time getting in there to skin the legs. After that, it's really just a matter of how far down the neck you can get the skin off before you cut the head off. Next, take your bone saw cut, all four legs off (if they're still there) and the head and you're done!

Aging

Now you're ready to age. Ensure when you cut the back legs, you do not cut the Achilles tendon, as that's what I used to hang the deer in the fridge. If you've sprayed the deer down with a hose, as you should to get all of the rest of the junk off, I would recommend patting down the meat and drying it off as best as possible before hanging it in the fridge. I keep a small thermometer in my fridge to try to keep the temperature between 36 and 39°. You should have the deer hanging while you're skinning it. The hardest part in the skinning process is trying to keep all the hair off the meat.

Before we talk about processing the meat let's cover a couple other options real quick. When I was stationed in 10th Special Forces Group I was fortunate to draw a first season elk tag for rifle. I had never killed an elk before and it was 100% a DIY Hunt. I didn't even know if there were any elk in my area. So, I got a tip from a guy that worked at Sportsman's warehouse, asked the buddy on my team to go with me, and we went. I really wanted to shoot an elk with a pistol, so I bought a Smith & Wesson .500 and was going to put a scope on it.

Unfortunately, while I was trying to zero it, the recoil was so bad it sheared the screws off, and the scope fell off! So, I bought a .300 win mag. The year was 2008 and first season elk tag usually meant the elk were still very high in the mountains as there was no snow to push them down.

I was a bit skeptical, but with the tip from the kind gentleman at *Sportsman's Warehouse*, off we went. The season was a weeklong and we were prepared to spend the whole week in the mountains. We went in a day early to set up camp and scout if we had time. We ended up with a couple hours of light left so we headed up the mountain to try some bugling and look for sign. We walked a mile or two up the mountain, bugled a bit, but didn't see or hear anything. We did see a bunch of old sign, but nothing too promising.

On our way back down the mountain there was a small field about a half a mile from camp just off of a small creek. To our surprise, we counted sixteen elk on this field, who were staring at us. We didn't have rifles, as we were just scouting. So, we just sat down and watched them. After about five minutes of watching this majestic spectacle, a 5 x 6 bull elk came prancing out from the woods through the field, as if saying, "These are my cows!" It was the coolest thing to see! It was almost dark and we watched them for about 15 minutes until they slowly moved off the field and into the timber. A part of me was devastated thinking we might not see those elk again, but it's hunting. You

6 – After the Kill

never know. So, we quietly made our way down to the creek and back to camp. As we sat around the campfire that night coming up with a plan, we were both super excited. Needless to say, neither one of us slept much that night. The plan was I would leave camp 30 minutes before him so I could get up to the field and get eyes on. He would push up from camp in the direction the elk moved and then moved to the field in hopes of pushing them to me. Little did we know, the elk were already on the field before I even left camp. And when I got there, still dark, I could see the shadowy figures out on the field. As soon as I noticed them, I melted into the ground, took off my pack, and waited for light. When it was light enough to see, I found my bull staring at me 150 yards away, facing directly towards me. I was staring at him in the scope, and he was staring back at me, both of us frozen in time.

Shooting light came and went, and the stare down continued. It was now about 14 minutes after shooting light, and a full 30 minutes from the time I hit the field. I could tell he was getting ready to move. I had my crosshairs on him, just waiting. When he turned and took his first step, I pulled the trigger. I hit a little higher and farther back than I would've liked, but the angle insured, my shot went through both lungs, and he fell dead, less than 20 yards from where I shot him.

I was probably the first person in Colorado in 2008 to harvest an elk. That was one of the best hunts of my life. I don't recall but we estimated he weighed around 800 pounds on the hoof. I was thinking, there's no way we are going to drag him anywhere. Luckily, my buddy used to be a guide in Alaska and had experience processing large animals. He cut and I walked. Six hours and 12 miles of walking later we had him back to camp. The point of the story is sometimes you have to cut up the animal while in the field. In this case we had packs and game bags ready. We cut all the meat off of the elk and left the entire carcass and all the bones minus the head and antlers. That was the last thing I carried out, and probably the hardest. His antlers measured 4 feet wide and 4 feet tall and with his head and hide attached was well over 100 pounds.

Another option would be to quarter the animal. This is simple enough. The quarters being the 4 legs. You can leave the skin on or not. Just don't forget the backstraps, inside tenderloins (like I did on my elk!), neck meat, and whatever else you want to take. Always get as much meat off the bone as you can. This is usually done at the kill site and then the meat gets wrapped in a game bag and put in packs to walk out. Deboning is also an option. Basically, the same as quartering, but also remove all bones. There are techniques for this to best get the meat off the bone without messing up your cuts. YouTube is a great resource.

I'd also like to go over dragging the whole animal. This is what I usually do as I'm never too far from my

6 – After the Kill

truck. The terrain here is generally flat. If it's a buck, grab an antler and start pulling. If it's a doe, grab a leg. If I'm pulling by a leg, I usually grab a back leg so the head is not flopping around. Be careful if you're pulling antlers, they're sharp and pointy! If you have a bad back like me, you can also invest in a deer sled, dragging straps, or any other method they sell.

Sometimes, when I'm hunting up at my lease and it's far back, I'll just strap it to the 4-wheeler and roll. I've used this method for carrying everything, especially if I don't have a 4-wheeler, and I'm back a ways, and don't want to walk two trips. Make a small incision on the back legs between the Achilles tendon and the main bone. Run a piece of cordage through and tie the other end around your waist. Carry everything else like normal and pull the deer.

Now, for the fun part! Taking this carcass out of the fridge and turning it into yummy steaks and burger! For all you butchers out there, please don't judge me. I haven't been perfecting my craft as I would like. I usually don't take the time to cut every cut of steak or roast out, and I usually just keep the back straps and tenderloins for steaks and turn the rest into burger. I'm not wasting meat as I still get as much as I can. I just end up with a lot of burger. Unless I keep anything out for jerky or maybe a roast. So, for simplicity sake, I will talk you through this method and if you want to learn more, I can include a link to a video that will discuss it in better detail.[4]

Backstraps

First, there's backstraps. This is by far my favorite part of the deer to eat. The backstraps are located next to the spine (about 3" wide depending on the size of the deer) from the base of the neck back to the base of the hind quarter. I like to cut this out with the deer hanging starting with a horizontal cut about 3 inches long at the base of the hindquarter. Then I trace the spinal cord down to the base of the neck and cut 3 inches out again. Going back to the top I now follow the bone of the spine to fill out the backstrap, repeat on the other side. Make sure to have a good boning knife when cutting up a deer. Trust me, it's worth it, and keep it sharp. The inside tenderloins are located on the pelvis at the bottom of the spine (inside the cavity). These can usually be pulled out with your hands, they're so tender.

Front Shoulders

Next, the front shoulders. If you haven't already cut the leg in half from the knee down, do so now. And if you haven't removed the hide yet, do so now. The shoulders are easily removed by pulling out on the leg and sticking your knife in the armpit of the deer and

---

[4] https://youtu.be/-r2ctQJJMsc?feature=shared

6 – After the Kill

cutting around the shoulder blade. The leg will easily come off. Repeat on both sides.

Hind Quarters

Hind quarters are a little more tricky. I recommend watching a tutorial video before you try it.[5] Also, remember, there is a lymph node in the center of the hind quarter. See the video which explains how to get it out. That will contribute to the gamey flavor as well so ensure you get all the lymph nodes out of the meat.

After you get your hind quarter cut up it's time to clean up the rest of the carcass. The neck will usually hold quite a bit of meat, so you'll just want to fillet it from around the spine. You can use it for a roast or ground. Now just get as much good meat off the bone as you can and put it in the ground pile. From here is packaging. I use either butcher paper or a vacuum sealer for the steaks. For the meat I'm going to grind, I'll freeze it for a month or two first. So, I'll just put it in a gallon Ziploc freezer bag. Once it's all packed up and in the freezer, time for clean up.

---

[5] https://www.instagram.com/wildgamecook/reel/CzsDKAVu37Y/

7

To the Table

"Behold, what I have seen to be good and fitting is to eat and drink and find enjoyment in all the toil with which one toils under the sun the few days of his life that God has given him, for this is his lot. Everyone also to whom God has given wealth and possessions and power to enjoy them, and to accept his lot and rejoice in his toil-this is the gift of God." (Ecclesiastes 5:18,19 ESV)

As the above Scripture testifies, God wants us to enjoy the food we've worked so hard to hunt and kill. I think one of the biggest benefits of being a deer hunter is

7 – To the Table

enjoying the fruits of my labor. And I do enjoy it. There are so many ways to prepare deer. Basically, anything you do with beef, you can do with deer. I want to take a second and point out the fact that I keep using the word deer and not venison. That's intentional.

According to Webster's, venison is "the edible flesh of a game animal and especially a deer." The term venison refers to the eating of any game animal. This is why I specify deer. Venison can mean elk, antelope, moose, caribou, beaver…..you get the point. Maybe it's just a pet peeve, much like how they count their points in the north versus the south. In the south you'll hear an 8 pointer whereas in the north you'll hear 4 by 4. In the north, you'll hear people say deer meat, whereas in the south, you'll hear people say venison. Both are correct, just helping you understand our different cultures within the United States regarding deer…. or venison.

The final phase of the Q-course, at least, when I went through, was SERE school (Survival, Evasion, Resistance and Escape). While I was in survival, which was about a week, they taught us various methods of hunting, trapping and fishing. The training included what to do and what not to eat in regards to the flora and fauna. During this survival week, you only got to eat what you found. As you can imagine, depending on the time of year, things are picked over pretty well. This being the case, I relied mostly on fishing. Even that was hard. I only caught one catfish. About halfway through the week one of the cadre hit a deer on the way to work and threw it in the truck and brought it in. We didn't get any meat, but he did offer up the liver to anyone who wanted it. To my surprise, no one else wanted it, so I got the whole thing. I was in hog heaven, so was my good friend Rodney, who was also an avid deer hunter. We ate like kings! We simply cut off small strips and roasted it on the campfire like a marshmallow. I knew it wouldn't last too long, so my plan was to eat it within a couple of days. The second day proved to be disastrous as I probably ate too much and got diarrhea. I don't think there was anything wrong with the meat. I just ate too much liver on an otherwise empty stomach. Not to mention the fact that I think I was hallucinating from drinking too much sassafras root tea! It was quite an experience. I'll never forget it, but at least I wasn't hungry. Not until evasion!

A few things about preparing food was covered in the previous chapter. Here however I want to discuss the preparation of the actual food.

A lot of the discussion has to do with the packing and storage of the meat itself, and how to properly prepare it for cooking. Disclaimer, I'm not a professional chef. So, cook the meat how you want. I'm only going to show you how to do it deliciously. I mean, I've only been stealing deer meat off the grill since I had teeth!

The first thing I want to talk about right away is something you'll probably hear from everyone who

7 – To the Table

doesn't eat deer meat. It's too gamey. The only thing I can say to this is that it's probably that person had some meat that wasn't properly prepared. If deer meat is prepared properly, it is some of the tenderest and most delicious meat you will ever eat. Please, please, please don't be that person that soaks your deer meat in vinegar or water to get out the gamey flavor. You will only ruin the meat. The fact of the matter is, how the meat tastes has a lot to do with what you do as a hunter from the moment you pull the trigger.

Details like, the temperature at the time of kill; how long the animal laid before you got the guts out; how long till the hide came off; the length of time until you had the deer hanging in a cooler; how long you leave it in the cooler; how you packaged the meat; how you stored the meat; how you prepared the meat; how you cut the meat; and finally how you cook the meat. So yes, great care has to be taken when processing a deer. Don't be afraid. Though nothing here is hard or difficult, there are just certain things you need to know and do and if done properly, the meat will not be gamey.

We've already talked about how long they can lay, gutting and skinning, and all of that, so I'd like to start off with packaging. I mentioned it in the last chapter but here are more details.

Other things that will make the meat gamey: silver skin (you'll see this in the butchering video, especially on the backstrap) connective tissue, fat, glands and hair. Care needs to be taken to remove all this while processing and only putting in the bag what you want to eat. Sometimes I'll leave the silver skin on the backstrap when I store it but I will remove it before I cook it. It's especially important to remove all the fat. Deer fat is typically where a lot of your gamey flavor will be. Once you have the meat cleaned up to your satisfaction, ensure whatever you're putting it in is freezer safe.

The bottom line is you don't want the meat to get freezer burned as it sits in your freezer all year. I use heavy duty freezer paper, and or freezer bags for the vacuum sealer. Also, ensure you mark each package with its contents and a date is always a good idea. Some people like to freeze their meat for a time before they eat any of it, but I will usually keep out a backstrap and eat it fresh, never frozen. Some people like to do this with the inside tenderloins as well.

Moving on to preparation and cooking tips.[6] Pull the pack of meat out of the freezer and place it in the fridge for a day or two to thaw. Once it's thawed, rinse the meat off with cold water, as it will most likely be a little bloody. Cut off or trim any excess silver skin, connective tissue, and fat that has remained. This only

---

[6] Here's a useful tutorial:
https://extension.umn.edu/preserving-and-preparing/cooking-venison-flavor-and-safety

7 – To the Table

applies to steak and roasts or other cuts as the burger will already be ready to eat.

Pro tip. Keep your steaks cut relatively thin, about a half inch to an inch. This is because steaks cook faster than beef. Not only that, but you can also pound it out to tenderize it as another cooking method. You'll see one of my recipes here soon. Marinating is another great option for deer meat. Also, just like beef, make sure your meat comes to room temperature prior to cooking. The biggest thing to remember when cooking deer is, it cooks faster than beef, so you really have to watch it. I like to eat my steaks at 140° so I'll pull them at 135° and let them rest for 10 minutes. You can do roasts in the crock pot or oven just like your grandma made them.

Remember, you can do the same thing with deer as you can with beef. Spaghetti, tacos, sloppy joes, SOS, stroganoff, burgers, meatballs. The list goes on. You get the idea.

Also, don't forget the organs! I failed to mention this in any previous chapter so I will mention it now. The heart, liver, kidneys and testicles are tasty too! Don't knock it till you try it. My son's favorite part of the deer is the heart. He loves my deer heart tacos. I really enjoy liver. Plus, I don't like to be wasteful. The animal has given its life for you, the least you can do is not waste anything. There are around 6 million deer killed every year by hunters, I can only imagine a lot gets wasted.[7]

Recipes

Recipes (chili, nuggets, stroganoff, chicken fried, bacon wrapped backstrap, deer heart tacos, jalapeño poppers, bone broth, marinade)

Food Type	Internal Temperature
Ground Beef, Pork, Veal & Lamb	160°F
Ground Turkey & Chicken	165°F
Chicken & Turkey, Whole	165°F
Poultry Parts	165°F
Ham Fresh (raw)	160°F
Ham Pre-Cooked (to reheat)	140°F

---

[7] Here is a link for help with cooking the organs. https://www.themeateater.com/cook/cooking-techniques/5-organs-you-should-save-from-deer

Holiday Meatballs

<u>Ingredients</u>:

1 lb. of deer sausage
½ large onion, finely chopped
1 cup shredded cheddar cheese
1 cup finely chopped dried cranberries
2 boxes of Stove Top stuffing (turkey)
1 cup of bone broth
2 large eggs
2 tbsp olive oil
½ cup water

<u>Dipping sauce</u>:

1 can whole berry cranberry
¼ cup orange juice

<u>Directions</u>:

1. Preheat oven to 375°.
2. Combine olive oil and water in a large skillet over medium heat. Add sausage and onions. Cook thoroughly. Place sausage and onions in a large bowl to cool for 10 minutes.
3. After mixture has cooled, add cheese, cranberries, and stuffing. Mix well.
4. Add eggs and broth. Mix well.
5. Roll mixture into hand size balls and place on cookie sheet.
6. Bake for 15 minutes.

Hoof to Table

Deer Chili

<u>Ingredients</u>:

1-2 lbs. deer burger
1 large yellow onion
1 can diced tomatoes
4 cans of beans with juice. Beans shooter's preference.
3 tbsp chili powder
2 tbsp cumin
1 tbsp garlic powder
1 tbsp onion powder
1 ½ tsp salt
½ tsp pepper
½ tsp cayenne pepper
1/8 cup brown sugar
1 bar of dark chocolate with cocoa

<u>Directions</u>:

1. Brown deer burger with onions.
2. Add to slow cooker. Then add all beans, diced tomatoes, chocolate bar and spices and mix well. Cayenne to preference.
3. Set slow cooker to 4 hours on high or 8 hours on low.
4. Add brown sugar at the end and serve.

Deer Stroganoff

Ingredients:

Deer backstrap
2 tbsp olive oil
Large onion
10 mushrooms
3 tbsp butter
1 package egg noodles
2 tbsp flour
2 cups bone broth
1 tbsp Dijon mustard
8 oz of sour cream
Salt and pepper

Directions:

1. Thinly slice and brown backstrap in olive oil over medium heat. Add salt and pepper. When cooked, set aside in bowl.
2. In a medium pan melt butter. Add onions. Cook for 1 minute. Add mushrooms. Cook until brown.
3. Add flour. Cook for 1 minute.
4. Slowly stir in bone broth. Bring to simmer. Cook for 5 minutes.
5. Prepare noodles.
6. Add backstrap to mixture.
7. Serve over noodles.

Hoof to Table

Chicken Fried Deer Nuggets

Ingredients:

1 lb. Deer backstrap
2 eggs
1 cup olive oil
1 cup flour
Panko breadcrumbs
1 ½ tsp salt
½ tsp pepper

Directions:

1. Slice backstrap into 1" slices/chunks.
2. In 3 separate containers add egg, flour and panko.
3. Heat oil to 350°.
4. Salt and pepper steak. Dip steak in flour first, then egg, then panko.
5. Fry until golden brown. 3-4 minutes per side.

7 – To the Table

Bacon Wrapped Backstrap

Ingredients:

1 backstrap, whole, trimmed
1 pound bacon
1 Tbsp olive oil
Salt and pepper

Directions:

1. Cover backstrap with oil, salt and pepper.
2. Lay bacon out on counter with pieces touching.
3. Place backstrap in center. Wrap bacon around and on with toothpicks.
4. Cook (preferably on smoker) at 225° until internal temperature reaches 135°.
5. Take off smoker and cover. Rest for 10 minutes and serve.

Jalapeño Poppers

Ingredients:

1 lb. Deer backstrap
2 Tbsp olive oil
1 ½ tsp salt
½ tsp pepper
12 jalapeños
1 pound bacon
1 package cream cheese
1 package ranch powder
1 cup shredded cheese

Directions:

1. Slice backstrap into 1" chunks/slices.
2. Bring a skillet to medium heat with olive oil. Salt and pepper deer meat and cook until done. Set aside.
3. Slice jalapeños in half and remove seeds. Set aside.
4. In a bowl; combine cream cheese, ranch and shredded cheese. Mix well.
5. Fill each jalapeño with a scoop of cheese mix, a piece of deer and wrap in bacon. Repeat until done.
6. Place jalapeños on smoker @ 350° until bacon is crispy.

Breakfast Sausage

Ingredients:

2 pounds deer sausage
2 tsp salt
1 1/2 tsp pepper
2 tsp sage
2 tsp thyme
1/2 tsp rosemary
1 Tbsp brown sugar
1/2 tsp nutmeg
1/2 tsp clove
1/2 tsp cayenne pepper
1/2 tsp red pepper flake

Hoof to Table

Deer Heart Tacos

<u>Ingredients:</u>

1 deer heart
1 packet taco seasoning (or homemade)
corn tortillas
1 white onion
Cilantro
lime

<u>Directions for taco seasoning:</u>

2 TBSP chili powder
1 TBSP Cumin
1 TBSP Garlic Powder
1 TBSP Onion Powder
1 TBSP Oregano
½ TBSP Paprika
1 tsp ground red pepper

<u>Directions:</u>

1. With a knife remove all the white tissue off the heart.
2. Cut it in half from top to bottom and clean out any remaining blood (steps 1 and 2 should be done before freezing).
3. Slice heart very thin going against the grain, no thicker than ¼ inch.
4. Season with salt and pepper.
5. Sear the heart in a cast iron pan with a tablespoon of oil, maybe a minute per side.
6. Sprinkle on a little bit of taco seasoning.
7. Serve on a corn tortilla with diced white onion and cilantro and a squeeze of lime.

Deer Bone Broth

Ingredients:

4 deer femur bones
2 cups chicken or beef broth
2 cups kale
1 large onion
2 cups carrots
2 cups celery

Directions:

1. Stack bones crosswise in a bottom crockpot.
2. Add all vegetables.
3. Add stock.
4. Add water to brim of crockpot.
5. Cook on high until boiling then turn to low.
6. Cook for 48 hours.
7. Strain liquid with sieve into mason jars.
8. Store in fridge or feezer.

8

Off Season

One of the main characteristics of being a hunter is a hunting drive. Hunting drive is determination. You have to want to go sit in the woods, even knowing you may not see anything. If you lack determination, hunting can be very frustrating at times. But as you should know by now, it can also be very rewarding. One morning in particular, a few years ago, I was going to go hunt up at my lease, but nobody else was free to go with me. Even though it's not the greatest idea, I do

8 – Off Season

hunt alone often. It's at these particular times I'm reminded why I hunt. I have a drive to hunt. And just because no one wants to go doesn't mean I can't.

So, when the alarm went off at 4 AM, I immediately got up and got to work. Made some coffee, grabbed a snack for after the hunt, gathered my gear, and headed out. I was especially excited because it was November, and the rut was on. I was going to my "secret spot" on the back corner of the lease where it meets up with the game lands. I arrived at the lease with plenty of darkness left to get in my tree. Gathered my gear, got on my 4-wheeler and headed in. I parked a couple hundred yards short of my stand and walked the rest of the way in with my climber and my rifle.

I decided to use estrous to see if I could get a passing buck to check it out. I forgot to put it on the far side of the hill, and based on the wind, I decided to put it on the same side as I was sitting. With the doe pee out, I climbed it into the tree, got settled and closed my eyes and waited for light. I still had a good hour before shooting light. About 20 minutes later, I heard two 4 wheelers off in the distance, coming onto the game lands. "Here we go!" I thought. About 20 minutes after that I heard some light crunching and was fairly certain a deer was approaching. I knew the squirrels weren't out yet. I could tell, whatever it was, it moving very cautiously. It kept getting closer and closer but because it was still dark, I couldn't see anything. It was right on top of me, close. All I could do was sit still and quiet and wait. I was fairly certain it was a buck as the sound was where I had put out the estrous doe pee. The problem now was, he had moved to my left, and 45° behind me. He was so close. I knew he would hear me move, but I also knew I had to be facing backwards if I wanted to have a shot. So, I took the next 20 minutes to slowly and carefully turn my body back to the left without making a sound. As time passed, the sky began to lighten. I could now see shadows, but still no deer, as he had been still for some time. Now I could see. Still nothing. What the heck did I hear? Now doubt began to set in and I'm wondering if it even was a deer or just some small critter rummaging around.

Still, I maintained my position and kept scanning. Unbeknownst to me there was a tree lower than me and was blocking the deer from my view. He took a step! It was a deer. And a nice 9 point at that! That deer stood still on top of my doe pee for almost an hour! He took another step and I fired. He was 15 yards from my tree. Dropped him in his tracks and my hunt was over at first light.

There can be a lot that goes into hunting up until the point of pulling the trigger. In this chapter, we will talk about all the things that happened during the off-season. Knowing these things will give you a better chance of harvesting deer. And I'm going to start with physical fitness. Being in shape is what allows me to hike into the woods with a climber on my back, sit in an uncomfortable position for hours, and then be able to drag a deer and all my gear back out of the woods successfully. Being in shape means something different to everyone. So, I don't need to spend too much time talking about this. If you're one of those people who are gray bearded like me, you already know where you're at and what you need to do. Botton line is, being physically fit will just make hunting easier for you. Personally, I've had wrist surgery, shoulder surgery, both of my knees have had surgery, and over the years have had multiple procedures on my back and neck. Staying in shape for me is a must. Find a program that works for you and stay in shape! Nothing will show your level of physical fitness like dragging dead weight over a distance.

Maintenance

Okay, you're in decent shape. What else do you do during the off-season? Well, this is where the real work starts. At my lease, we meet twice a year, early spring and late summer. Most of the time is spent reposting property boundaries, making sure the roads are clear, checking treestands, clearing shooting lanes, maintaining game cams and keeping an eye on everything, putting up new stands or moving old ones. You get the idea. Things wear down, things break, and they need to be maintained. A person doesn't realize how worn-down things can get until you leave them out in the elements 24/7, 365.

As we move through this chapter, try not to get overwhelmed. Remember, this is a group of guys that have been hunting their whole lives, and who have acquired a ton of gear throughout the years. If you're new to this, be patient. It takes time to acquire all these skills.

For starters, there's clearing the land. Obviously, if you hunt mostly public land, this isn't something you would do. Unless you plan on leaving your stand up on public land or maybe clearing some shooting lanes. But the stuff I'm talking about here is mainly for private property. If you do plan on leaving a standup on public land, make sure you're aware of the rules and regs for your state. It's also probably a good idea to throw a chain around your stand and put a padlock on it to prevent sticky fingers. Locks keep honest men honest!

The first thing we do is drive all the roads with ATVs to ensure the roads are clear. We have chainsaws, pole saws, hedge clippers, and handsaws. We may need to use a winch on an ATV to move a big tree. One of the guys also has a tractor with a bush hog so if anything grows up too crazy, we can mow it all down. Once that is done, we check treestands. What you're looking for here is to make sure the treestand is still serviceable, but mainly you're checking that the straps haven't rotted. If they are, they need to be replaced. It's probably a good idea to replace them every few years anyways, depending on the type of strap you're using.

8 – Off Season

You also need to check buckles and pads if they have them. This would also be a good time to wrap any exposed metal with tape or pads to aid in silencing your stand. This is also a good time to move any stands you want to move or put up any new stands. Once all the stands are done and checked, next is clearing shooting lanes, this involves multiple people. One guy will climb up and sit in the treestand and direct someone on the ground with a pole saw to trim any branches in order to create shooting lanes. Keep in mind if you're doing this early spring, more than likely, it will need to get done again before season starts. Things grow through the summer. Remember, the deer don't do the same thing every year exactly so pay attention to your game cam pics and the deer sign on the ground when you're moving stands. There are pros and cons to this.

I think the deer get used to the stands that are left in the same place for a long time. But I think it's also a con because the mature bucks will probably avoid those areas, especially during the daylight. Once that is complete, it's unlikely to get all of that done in one day, we would call that good.

There are still plenty of things to consider, however. Do you have any new gear? Well, now would be the time to practice with it. Use the off-season to get familiar with anything new so you're familiar with it when you're using it for real. Use the same process with your gear that you did for your stands. Check everything out for serviceability. Clean it. Replace anything that's broken. Silence it if it needs to be silenced, or simply replace it.

Just a quick example of not taking care of your gear. Remember here in the southeast our summers get hot and humid. Once November hits, I usually put the bow away so I can get the freezer full. This year I completely forgot about my bow and focused on rifle hunting. I put my bow in the case, threw it in the garage and forgot about it. One lazy weekend I decided to pull my bow out and shoot just for some practice. When I opened the case, I found my entire bow covered in mold. It must've been a bit damp or humid when I put it away and I let it sit for a month or so. That's on me. I let $1500 worth of gear sit and mold because I didn't take the time to put it up and clean it when I was done. Don't be like me! Of course, I got it cleaned up with some bleach water and nothing was damaged but that's not the point. I spend a lot of money on this stuff, and I want to take care of my gear.

Maintaining food and supplements throughout the year can be essential for keeping deer on your land. A lot of professionals will do this by planting food plots throughout the year. The deer have everything they need when they need it. If you were able to do this more power to you, I am not. I simply rely on the fact that the deer will be there next year! Any guidance you need on maintaining food plots throughout the year will have to be another book. However, game cams is another story.

8 – Off Season

You can absolutely maintain an eye on your land, year around by checking your cameras. This will tell you what deer are still in the area, if they're still in the area, what they're doing, or whatever else you're looking for. It's also fun to see when the bucks shed their antlers and then watching them grow back. That leads me to another fun activity, shed hunting.

Personally, I've not had much luck in the past, but that doesn't deter me. If nothing else, it's just another reason to get out in the woods in the spring. Deer season is never over! Apparently, there's a science to finding these hard-to-find trinkets, but I won't bore you with those details here. A quick internet search can give you some pointers on where to look. But basically, look where the bucks are. Bedding areas, travel corridors, and my favorite tip is places they jump, like fences or creeks. The jumping has a tendency to knock their antlers off when they're close to falling off. They're hard to find but it's fun to look nonetheless.

Now, while you're doing everything mentioned in this chapter, you're also doing something else that you didn't even realize. Recon or scouting. Now is the time to check out that corner of your property that you've always wanted to look at, or you remember seeing a buck traveling a certain way and had never been down there and want to see where he might be going. You get the idea.

Of course this is all on your own land. But if you're cruising your own land, take some time to learn it. If you have OnX you can mark bedding areas, food sources, water sources, travel corridors, scrapes and rubs. As well as all your treestand locations as well as cameras. One thing I haven't mentioned yet is creating wildlife habitat. This is a whole other subject. I don't have any expertise in it, so I won't add too much here. You'll have to research this one on your own if you would like to try it. Basically, there is a way of felling trees in certain areas that will actually create bedding areas and safe spaces for deer to hang out. You can also use manmade fallen trees to create funnels to try and dictate their movement.

Another type of recon I use is with my app, OnX. That's how I was able to find the location of my big 10 point I shot this year. Use map recon to find an area, then go out, boots on the ground, and start from square one. It never ends, and that's another driving force that keeps me going. There's always something you can do year-round that pertains to deer hunting. If all else fails, you can always try the old-fashioned door knocking technique. I haven't done too much of this lately and more than likely depends on where you live and the views of hunting in your area. But it can't hurt to ask, the worst they can say is no. If you do get a yes, though, remember to be polite and courteous to their rules as you're hunting on their land. I consider this a great honor and always offer to help in any way I can to return the favor.

9

On the Range

This is by far my favorite deer hunting story of all time. On this particular hunt, Frank Cole, my best deer hunting buddy went along. I had the privilege to serve with him as an SUT instructor. We have shared many deer hunting trips together. He is a true warrior and the only person that I know that hunts like I do. Now, bow hunting is hard enough. You have to get close to your prey. When your prey is whitetail deer that doesn't make it an easy task. This was a bowhunting trip. We picked out a spot to "double hunt." We hunted in the same area and sat about 100 yards apart. It was a small piece of game lands just outside of Camp Mackall. We've hunted it several times before and had killed some pretty nice bucks in there.

There was a trail that went off of the backside of a field into the thick woods. The trail was shaped like a lightning bolt, I sat at the first bend, Frank at the second. About 8:30 in the morning on opening day of bow season, a small buck walked off the field straight to me. Now being the smart hunter I was, I put my climber on the backside of the tree so if anything walked off the field, I would have the tree between me and it. It seemed like a good idea at the time, but as I drew my bow to take the shot, I quickly realized the tree was in my way.

As I leaned to my left to get a clear shot, the top of my treestand slipped off the tree, and I nearly fell out of the stand (I didn't have a harness on). As I slipped, I fired my bow. The arrow landed straight in the dirt. Luckily, I didn't fall out of the tree, but even more luckily, the deer hopped a couple steps and stopped. So, I notched another arrow and let her fly. Initially, I thought I missed because the deer hopped off again, stood there for a moment, and then casually walked away. He popped out on the other side of the trail, headed toward Frank. So, I gave my typical "meh" sound, stopping the deer at 25 yds, and shot again. Again, I didn't realize I had hit him (I wasn't using luminoks) and he casually walked away.

A few minutes after he rounded the corner, I could hear Frank firing his bow three times as well over a period of a couple minutes! I had no idea what was happening. So, I texted him and he confirmed we had

9 – On the Range

a downed deer. Once I got down on the ground and found the deer, I realized that I hit him with two arrows. Frank hit him with three! The blood trail indicated a vital hit. As I stated before, it's hard enough to get one shot with a bow on a deer before they run away. We just shot this deer five times with bow and arrows!

That story is a clear indication of how tough these animals really are, and why we owe them our best to kill them as quickly and humanely as possible. This requires us, as hunters, to be on our "A" game. I mentioned in the last chapter about staying physically fit in some way, but I'd like to go a little deeper here.

Part of your gym routine should include strength and endurance training. In reference to the story above, had I been out of shape, I could have fallen out of the tree, and gotten severely injured, or even killed. Now, I know what you're thinking, you should've had your safety harness on dummy! I will say you are absolutely right. But I've had other situations where I was climbing a tree with a climber, and it wasn't tied together properly. The bottom portion fell down farther than I could reach, and had I not been able to do a pull up, that could have been worse. Point being, make sure you can get yourself out of whatever situation you put yourself into, physically.

How comfortable are you with being uncomfortable? As a hunter you may find yourself holding uncomfortable positions for a long time in order to take a shot. You may find yourself moving through some rough terrain that requires a great deal of physical fitness over long distances. You may find yourself with a 200-pound animal that you have to drag a half a mile back to your truck. I think you get the idea. Get comfortable being uncomfortable. This just gives me all the more reason to find things to do outside during the off-season. There are plenty of outdoor activities to keep busy such as hiking, fishing, camping, and shed hunting. Try to make these activities a part of your regular off-season.

This is where having served 20 years in the Army pays off! The ARSOF core attributes are integrity, courage, perseverance, personal responsibility, professionalism, adaptability, team player, and capability. Take a minute and ponder how these attributes can directly relate to hunting. What about discipline, humility, being self motivated, commitment? You've heard these all before, but do you apply them? Now you have the opportunity to use the skills God has given you to be successful in other areas of life, and not just hunting. But that's a different book. So how does this look? Let's start with range time. Let's face it, after about an hour of shooting (bow or rifle) you're about done. And how often do you get range time?

I understand it's not feasible to shoot every day, but find your routine. It's easy to get bored or burnt out on

9 – On the Range

range time. Mix up your routine, make a schedule and stick to it (commitment). Range time is a necessary evil. You have to do it if you want to retain your skill. As we all know, if you don't use it, you lose it! Practice shooting in nonstandard shooting positions. A mistake some bowhunters make is just to stand on level ground and shoot straight forward at 20, 30, and 40 yds. Now I'm not saying don't do this because it is very good practice. But we need to train like we fight. So, get in your stand, bring your climber and practice. Shoot from an elevated position, shooting around objects or on a knee or any other position you can think of you may find yourself in in the woods.

During my time as an SUT instructor, I had the privilege of being surrounded by a lot of bowhunters. We used to all bring our bows to work, and at lunchtime would go out in the woods and take turns getting in a treestand while the other person would move the target around to different distances and positions. We would practice known and unknown distance shooting. This was very helpful, and fun. Of course, all the trash talk helps too.

Another way to stay sharp during the off-season is small game hunting. Here in North Carolina rabbit and squirrel season stays open till the end of February so you still have a couple months after deer season ends to stay in the woods. Plus, on private land, there is no closed season for small game, or bag limit! These include groundhog, nutria, coyote, striped skunk, armadillo, and wild hog. I can assure you nothing will keep your skills sharper than hunting, coyotes and wild hogs.

Last year me and two buddies decided to go down to Fort Stewart, Georgia, and try some hog hunting. We all drove down separately, met up on a Friday night, pitched a tent at a campground, and prepped our gear. We hunted all day Saturday and half day Sunday before returning home. Unfortunately for us, it rained most of Saturday, so hunting was hard. We didn't really have a plan other than drive around till we saw some hogs and then try to stalk them. We walked around quite a bit too, looking for fresh sign. We contemplated hunting from climbers on fresh sign, but we just didn't have a lot to go on.

We happened upon a sow crossing a dirt trail Saturday afternoon and I made easy work of her with my AK-47. She was the only pig we killed. It was, however, a blast! We saw the biggest timber rattlesnake I've ever seen! We even had an alligator try to sneak up on us while we were resting by a small pond. Now, I think we're going to make it an annual trip. We'll do more homework and hopefully figure out a better strategy for getting on some pig. They are very good eating, and I can't wait to go back.

Bottom line is don't get complacent. Stay sharp. Get organized. Go outside and enjoy creation. But don't just focus on shooting. Don't forget about all your other

9 – On the Range

gear. If you haven't cleaned it from last season, get it out. Clean it. Take batteries out of things that are going to sit. You should also be using your gear while you're out shooting. This is a perfect opportunity to practice using all the gadgets and perfecting them. Again, don't forget about the dark. You should know how to operate all your equipment in the dark, efficiently.

10

The Morality of Killing

"Now then, take your weapons, your quiver and your bow, and go out to the field and hunt game for me," (Genesis 27:3 ESV)

"But ask the beasts, and they will teach you; the birds of the heavens, and they will tell you; or the bushes of the earth, and they will teach you; and the fish of the sea will declare to you. Who among all these does not know that the hand of the LORD has done this? In his hand is the life of every living thing and the breath of all mankind" (Job 12:7, ESV).

It's important to understand the truth of the Word of God when making any decision in life. This is especially

10 – The Morality of Killing

important when it comes to taking a life. The sixth commandment is "You shall not murder" (Exodus 20:13). This commandment bans the illegal taking of human life. This commandment does not refer to animals. Bottom line, according to the Bible, it is not a sin to kill animals as long as it's for consumption or protection and it's done as humanely as possible.

In 2001, I was stationed in Fort Richardson, Alaska. If there was ever a sportsman's paradise, this was it. Unfortunately for me I was in my early 20's and alcohol was a new experience for me which took up more of my time than I would have liked. I did get to experience salmon and halibut fishing, but was only able to do a few hunts. These consisted of bear, moose and caribou. I was not successful. I saw plenty of game while I was there but never while I was hunting. The reason I bring this up is because I knew a guy who apparently got a kick out of poaching. He claimed to have shot and killed a bald eagle and even a large mature bull moose. Now I'm not sure exactly what a person like this is thinking but he obviously has no respect for God's creatures. "Whoever is righteous has regard for the life of his beast, but the mercy of the wicked is cruel." (Proverbs 12:10 ESV).

I cannot say I've never poached, I'm not proud of it, but God gave me better sense than that, and my dad taught me the right way. I now only kill what I eat. I shot birds when I was a kid and probably other small critters. That was wrong of me to do but I'd like to think that God used that in my life as a future way to honor Him. Now, I can teach my son, and others, the truth in killing animals. This is a very controversial topic amongst hunters, but I think the bottom line is, we have to respect all God's creatures as well as the land we're hunting.

Let me pose a question: Can you respect the animal but still break the law? Therein lies the question, is it still morally right even if it's against the law. That may seem like a contradiction but hear me out. As I'm writing this chapter, I'm sitting in a treestand. I shot a deer about an hour and a half ago, midday, but was planning on hunting till dark. A buddy of mine said he'd tag it so I could keep hunting. He came out and tagged the deer and took it home, I returned to my tree. Two and half hours later, from the same tree, I shot a big 3 ½- 4 ½ year old six pointer. Is that illegal, technically yes. Is it morally wrong, I don't think so. Did I respect the animal? Absolutely! My buddy tagged it and ate it. My dad taught me the right way, as I will teach my son, and we all make our own decisions. Mine are between me and God. I think there are hunters out there that would call me a hypocrite, and this would enrage them. To them I will say this. I respect all animals I encounter, and I eat everything I kill.

Think about this. Somewhere out there, are high fenced and "managed" deer. There are a lot of rich people out there with a lot of land and they charge ridiculous fees for people to "hunt." How can one say

10 – The Morality of Killing

that's morally right when you can almost guarantee the big one will come in when the feeder goes off. That's not hunting! That's shooting "tame" deer in a fence. And yet, that's perfectly legal! I feel like I could go on another tangent here about the state of the world and rising inflation, especially the cost of meat. However, I'm providing meat for me and mine. I am in no way justifying any illegal actions, just explaining my thought process. And in no way am I condoning breaking the law. The laws are intended to keep hunters and bystanders safe, as well as effectively manage game through conservation efforts.

All I'm saying is what everyone else is already thinking, just because it's morally wrong, doesn't mean it's illegal and just because it's morally right, doesn't mean it's legal. As it is said, "Animal cruelty should not take place if men truly understand the command to be 'caretakers' of the earth." We are to control the numbers of animals so disease and sickness do not kill them off. We are to use the animals for our needs. We are to control animals in a manner in which they are not harmful to human, and we should protect them from over-killing and abuse. The problem lies in the fact that many do not understand this balance and tend to over-protect or under-protect animals. Animals were created for us to enjoy, so protecting a remnant for others to enjoy is also proper.

I think the thing I like most about being a father is when all the little moments along the way happen, and then realizing my father experienced those same moments years and years ago. I don't think you realize when you're a kid everything your parents go through at an adult level. Kids are lazy and selfish by nature. Let's face it, they're just too young to understand how the world works. I see this all too well in my nine-year-old son. Even explaining to him some of my dealings with the war in Iraq or explaining to him how there are children in Africa who don't get to eat every day or have clothes to wear.

Now, don't get me wrong, my son has a heart of gold and loves to help people, but he just doesn't understand the world yet. His mom loves animals and hunting was always a fight when we were married. I can see how this is confusing for him. Ultimately, he will have to make his own decision as to whether or not he decides to hunt. I was in my 30s when I heard that my dad would go out at night with a .22 mag and a spotlight and shoot deer down by the river just so we had meat to eat. Is that legal? Nope. Do I think any less of my dad for that? Nope. He did what he had to do to provide for his family at the time.

Now we could probably get into a theological debate here, but the bottom line is, he'll have to answer to God for what he did, and no one else. Just like my buddy in Alaska will have to answer for everything he did, and I'll have to answer for everything I did. Bottom line, we have been given a duty, by God, to care for all creation.

10 – The Morality of Killing

If we use His Word as our guide, we can enjoy His creation for all He intended it for.

"Every moving thing that lives shall be food for you. And as I gave you the green plants, I give you everything." (Genesis 9:3 ESV)

11

The Next Generation

"We have fallen heirs to the most glorious heritage a people ever received, and each one must do his part if we wish to show that the nation is worthy of its good fortune." – Theodore Roosevelt

One of the current hunting opportunities I have is a lease in Montgomery County, North Carolina. It sits just outside Candor and consists of about 300 acres. One fall, during the rut, my son Teagan and I went out in hopes of taking a "nice buck" running around out there. We sat in a double ladder stand on a hilltop. About an hour before dark the magic happened. From behind me and to my right, I heard a rustling of leaves, I turned my head just in time to see a buck chasing a

The Next Generation

doe. It wasn't a monster but definitely a shooter. That doe ran by at full speed and never slowed down. I desperately tried to stop the buck with a grunt, but he paid me no attention. They were about 75 yds from us and continued over the hill and ran out of sight. I peered through the trees and listened, but they were gone. To our surprise the doe, for whatever reason, came running back the exact line they can in on. This time, I was ready! As they came running back by I tried grunting again and when that didn't work I went for the running shot, not the best option of course. But they were only about 75 yds, and I knew it was my only option.

Me and my son Teagan.

My first shot was a clean miss, but it stopped him in his tracks. I quickly worked the bolt and fired a lethal shot, behind the front shoulder. I explained to Teagan we had to give him time before we got down. About 20 minutes later, I already heard him crash, we got down and I let Teagan follow the blood trail the short 50 yards to where he laid. We said a quick prayer, thanking the Lord for providing us meat, and went back for the 4-wheeler.

One of the great privileges I have is the opportunity to take my son hunting. I do this in the hope that one day he will carry on the tradition with his son. He's not taking a great interest in it at present. I'm also doing my best not to push him too hard. I've had him in a tree with me the last two or three years and his biggest complaint is sitting in a treestand is boring. I get it. I didn't grow up hunting this way, and quite honestly, I don't care for it either. However, hunting in the southeastern U.S., that's how I've found to be most successful. So as time moves forward, I will do my best to encourage him to keep coming. I'll keep taking him shooting during the off season, in hopes he will one day harvest his own deer.

I got a chance to take my son and my girlfriend's son hunting this year too. I knew before we left, we probably wouldn't see any deer but if they wanted to go, I was taking them. I put them both in a double ladder stand with specific instructions to sit still and be quiet. They're both nine. I then got in my climber in a tree beside them. We sat for about an hour and a half but neither of them could sit still for more than 10 seconds. To my demise, I showed my frustration more than I should have. But on the way home I stopped at the store and got them both a piece of pizza and a Yoo Hoo and just explained that hunting takes patience, and we'd try again another time. I have great hopes they will take to it but, if not, I will continue to enjoy my passion.

For context and awareness, I want to briefly talk about how hunters are currently the main contributors to wildlife conservation and how that came about. Theodore Roosevelt was the first president of the 1900's. This was a pivotal time in our United States history due to the fact that over hunting was about to wipe out most of the big game including buffalo, elk, and deer. He was an avid sportsman and loved the outdoors and hunting. He saw the writing on the wall which was why he became known as the conservation president.

During his time as president, he used his power to create the United States Forest Service (USFS) as well as establish 150 national forests, 51 federal bird reserves, 4 national game preserves, 5 national parks and 18 national monuments by enabling the 1906 American Antiquities Act.

Roosevelt knew that nature existed to benefit man. He knew it had to be protected. He grew up in a time I wish I could have seen this country, before the stain of man spilled haphazardly about. As a child he traveled abroad with his family to Egypt where he hunted and mounted birds. He kept detailed records of all the wildlife he found and killed for study. He always had a passion for it. I personally believe if it wasn't for what he did, this country would look a whole lot different today.

So, what does it look like today? Today it's called the Theodore Roosevelt Conservation Partnership. In 2014, it donated 84% of the 3.7 million in revenue to conservation programs. This is just the tip of the iceberg. The Rocky Mountain Elk Foundation donates 91%, Ducks Unlimited donated a whopping 84% of 2 billion dollars of its expenditures. But wait, there's more. There are 13,950 wildlife protection organizations in the United States. Combined they provide employment for 20,088 people, earn more than $5 billion in revenue annually and have assets of $10 billion.

I know this all sounds great but if you're asking yourself, "Well, what does that have to do with me?" Well obviously, if you're the type of person who likes donating, then, now you know how you can help. If not, don't worry, approximately 80% of funds at the state level are generated by hunters and anglers. When you buy your state hunting and fishing license, a portion goes directly to conservation programs in your state. In FY21, North Carolina alone collected $39 million in

The Next Generation

license sales. So, we can clearly see that conservation efforts are in place and working. Just remember, there's always an opposition. They're working just as hard to get "our" land for shopping malls and parking garages so we must fight to keep it. [8]

---

[8] https://www.nps.gov/thro/learn/historyculture/theodore-roosevelt-and-conservation.htm
https://www.causeiq.com/directory/wildlife-protection-organizations-list/
https://www.ncwildlife.org/Connect-With-Us/Blog/where-do-license-dollars-go#:~:text=When%20you%20buy%20a%20license,we%20can%20achieve%20those%20efforts.

Conclusion

Deer hunting has changed a lot in my lifetime. Some people are made famous because of it. Me, I'm just a guy who likes to hunt deer. I'm nobody special. I'm not rich or famous. I don't own land. I simply love the thrill of the hunt. Everything in this book is my opinion. But it's also based on my experience. Everything regarding preparation, clothing, tactics, etc. I've learned from experience. Some of the technical data I researched from the internet, but 90% of the information came out of my head. What inspired me to write this book was a desire to help a friend get back into hunting. The book grew out of the instruction I gave him.

Around the second or third hunt we did, my friend jokingly stated, "Man you ought to write a book!" That struck a chord. One thing I learned about myself in the

Conclusion

military is I love teaching. This is why I still do what I do. But I've never taught hunting before. A little bit with my son, but never an adult. Teaching keeps me sharp; it makes me realize what I've taken for granted. It also made me realize that not everyone grew up with a father who took them hunting. This point has turned into the main reason for writing this book.

Anyone out there, anyone who wants to get into hunting can and should go for it. To all my veteran brothers out there, if you're struggling, if you feel like you've lost your purpose, or just need a new hobby, hunting might be for you!

I've told a lot of stories of killing deer. And I have killed a lot of deer... in the hundreds. I'm not saying this to brag, only to show how passionate I am about it. You may not be as successful at first. Be patient. Be persistent. No one starts out as an expert. I hesitate to even call myself an expert now. Perhaps I'm simply experienced. I've just learned from countless hunting trips and countless misses and failures. But that's the excitement. I didn't kill a deer with my bow until I was 30. You don't kill deer every time you go hunting. A lot of times you don't even see a deer. I can remember going five or six times in a row without seeing a single deer. It shouldn't be about the killing. Do it for something else. Something in you. I love it. Every year I get excited about deer season. And every year, every time the first deer of the season steps out I get buck fever! And that is the reason I keep doing it. Find your reason. I hope you get the same excitement out of it as I do. Then most importantly, pass it on to someone else. My first love goes out to the good Lord Almighty. Second, my family, followed by a close third, deer hunting. But don't do it for the killing. Learn how to be a good sportsman. Enjoy God's creation. Take care of the earth. We are to care for ALL God's creation. Happy hunting! I love you all, God bless.

"So, whether you eat or drink, or whatever you do, do all to the glory of God" (1 Corinthians 10:31, ESV).

About the Author

Brandon Reil was born and raised in Montana. After graduating high school in 1998, he joined the US Army, and served with the 3rd Ranger Battalion, the 1/501st Parachute Infantry Regiment, the 10th Special Forces Group (A), and the John F. Kennedy Special Warfare Center and School. Since his 20-year career, Brandon continues to serve as a contractor for various parts of the Special Forces Qualification Course (SFQC). His passion is deer hunting.

Check out the background to his book on the Pinelander Podcast, Episode 089: The Deer Hunter. December 22, 2023.

https://www.podbean.com/wlei/pb-ayk4g-152ce01

Photo Gallery

Montana, 1992. First deer

Hoof to Table

Cottontail Creek, Montana, 1993. Second deer.

Photo Gallery

Raspberry Mountain, Colorado, 2008.

Hoof to Table

Camp Mackall, North Carolina, 2011.

Photo Gallery

Camp Mackall, North Carolina, 2011.

Camp Mackall, North Carolina, 2013. Bow.

Photo Gallery

"Lee Harvey." Montgomery County, North Carolina, Dec 2023.

Hoof to Table

Richmond County, North Carolina, November 2023.

Photo Gallery

Moore County, North Carolina, November 2020.

Hoof to Table

North Carolina, Dec 2020.

Photo Gallery

Montgomery County, November 12, 2022.

Hoof to Table

Moore County, North Carolina, Nov 2020.

Photo Gallery

Camp Mackall, North Carolina, Nov 2023.

Kentucky, Nov 2019.

Connect with Blacksmith Publishing

www.blacksmithpublishing.com

Printed in the USA
CPSIA information can be obtained
at www.ICGtesting.com
CBHW030726180824
13256CB00047B/482